Your insight was
development of.
Thank you for everything.

Denise Armstrong
June, 2010

MW01539037

ADMINISTRATIVE PASSAGES

STUDIES IN EDUCATIONAL LEADERSHIP

VOLUME 4

SCOPE OF THE SERIES

Leadership we know makes all the difference in success or failures of organizations. This series will bring together in a highly readable way the most recent insights in successful leadership. Emphasis will be placed on research focused on pre-collegiate educational organizations. Volumes should address issues related to leadership at all levels of the educational system and be written in a style accessible to scholars, educational practitioners and policy makers throughout the world.

The volumes – monographs and edited volumes – should represent work from different parts in the world.

For further volumes:
http://www.springer.com/series/6543

ADMINISTRATIVE PASSAGES

Navigating the Transition from Teacher to Assistant Principal

by

DENISE E. ARMSTRONG

Brock University, St. Catharines, Ontario, Canada

🜸 Springer

Denise E. Armstrong
Brock University
Faculty of Education
St Catharines ON L2S 3A1
Canada
Denise.armstrong@brocku.ca

ISBN 978-1-4020-5268-2   e-ISBN 978-1-4020-5269-9
DOI 10.1007/978-1-4020-5269-9
Springer Dordrecht Heidelberg London New York

Library of Congress Control Number: 2009929299

Printed on acid-free paper

Springer is part of Springer Science+Business Media (www.springer.com)

This book is dedicated to my parents Cynthia and Joseph Forde and my in-laws Paula and Bill Armstrong.

Foreword

This book makes a much needed contribution to what we know about the role and work of the assistant principal. It offers terrific insights into the different challenges one faces after being appointed assistant principal, and it provides readers with a rich array of data regarding the mental, emotional, social, and physical adjustments accompanying one's transition to this new role.

The author refreshingly moves beyond mere description of what assistant principals do as they make their transition to that role, and actually helps us gain a sense of *the lived experience of becoming and being an assistant principal.* The book gives a realistic picture of the cognitive, social, and emotional conflicts and confusions, the daily ups and downs, the fears, frustrations, and highs that are experienced by the men and women undertaking the passage from teaching to administration.

This book is distinctive for a number of reasons. It is an empirical study of the role of the assistant principal. There are comparatively few helpful studies, and Professor Armstrong's research adds a solid and much needed addition to that body of work. It focuses on the transition from being a teacher to being an assistant principal, and it reveals much about how the assistant principal's role transition differs markedly from that of the school principal. In focusing on the adjustments and adaptations a newcomer to the assistant principal position must make, it provides the reader with valuable data regarding the psychological and socio-emotional as well as cognitive effects of the transition experience on the assistant principal. The viewpoint reflected is that of the assistant principal undergoing this change in roles. Finally, it offers a clear and well-conceptualized theoretical framework for describing and understanding the key variables and significant interactions that shape the transition from one's work and responsibilities as a teacher to the new challenges and generally unfamiliar terrain of the assistant principal's world.

Through interviews with eight assistant principals in a large school district, the researcher vividly captures a sense of the lived experience of becoming and being a new assistant principal. The author's descriptions of the emotional, social, and cognitive challenges, frustrations, and adjustments these men and women experience provide rich understandings of what assistant principals actually feel and think as they strive to understand and adapt to their new set of responsibilities. While most studies of administrator socialization focus on the externals, the behaviors of the individual, this study focuses on the internals, the emotional and psychological dynamics being experienced by the individual undergoing the transition.

In describing the process of identity development accompanying the transition from teaching to the assistant principalship, Professor Armstrong richly describes the impact of this journey on those undertaking this passage, identifying as well the major sources of role strain and the impact of those pressures on the novice assistant principal. These assistant principals' stories allow us to get inside their heads and hearts and to learn what they value and how they make decisions and adjust to their situations. As noted earlier, this attention to the assistant principal's internal thoughts and feelings, a neglected research arena, is a central feature of this work and is one of its most important contributions.

Beyond offering readers a reality-based glimpse into the emotional world of the person making the transition to this role, the author's research also pinpoints and describes key aspects of the terrain of the assistant principalship, helping us understand the pressures and frustrations many new assistant principals must cope with and adjust to as they strive to be successful in the role. While we already know a little about these features of the landscape from earlier studies, the book's major contribution is in helping us understand the nature of the cognitive, psychological, and socio-emotional impacts on the assistant principal of the stresses and strains experienced by the person undergoing this transition. Listed below are some of the aspects of the situations in which these novice assistant principals find themselves, and to which they must adjust:

- Leaving membership in the teacher group, yet not fully being embraced by or identifying psychologically as a member of the administrator group – feeling like they don't belong anywhere;
- Feeling caught in the middle of different pressures from all sides, being expected by all parties to solve all presented problems, and to have a working grasp of all the systems in place – and not having the formal or local knowledge to do so;
- Dealing with a much more complex and extensive array of stakeholders and roles – other than was the case in one's role as a teacher;
- Needing to gain the trust and establish effective social relations with teachers, particularly veteran teachers – all the while being viewed with suspicion by the teaching staff;
- Experiencing unanticipated feelings of loss and isolation – and feeling bullied and intimidated by parents and veteran teachers;
- Being undermined by superiors' overturning of their decisions – and feeling powerless; and
- Concurrently deconstructing one's previous notions of the assistant principalship role, relinquishing one's former teacher identity, and forging a new sense of oneself as an assistant principal.

These unanticipated stresses and strains have emotional and psychological consequences for new assistant principals as they seek to adjust and adapt themselves to their new circumstances as an administrator. Assistant principals' role passages are further complicated not just by the shift in identity from teacher reference group to administrator reference group, but in these times in particular there are many additional stressors in the context of contemporary schools and communities – increasing rules and regulations, increasing pressures for efficiency, and increasingly changing community and student demographics, in suburban as well as in urban school districts.

Contributing substantially to our empirical understanding of this transition process, its critical features, and the impact on the person undertaking this passage, Professor Armstrong offers an empirically grounded theoretical framework that identifies the key concepts and their interrelationships that powerfully capture and enable one to understand the various cycles of this role passage, the manner in which these cycles interact one with another, and their meaning for the assistant principal undergoing this role transition.

Drawing on socialization and identity development theory and research from various fields, Professor Armstrong constructs a role transition/identity development model. It includes four cycles of development that interact and build one upon another. She identifies four epicycles of transition. These include Entry-Exit, Immersion-Emersion, Disintegration-Reintegration, and Transformation-Restabilization. The model is solidly grounded in her charting of the personal, professional, and organizational paths traveled by novice assistant principals as they move from teaching into unfamiliar administrative terrain. It further clarifies for us the cognitive, emotional, and behavioral processes the assistant principals experience, and the adaptations and adjustments they find they must make as they strive to succeed in the role.

In addition to its usefulness for prospective assistant principals, university preparation program faculty, researchers studying school administration, senior school district administrators, and school principals also will find a great deal of the information helpful in facilitating and supporting a successful role transition for the assistant principal. Ironically, the experiences of the assistant principals reported and analyzed here, although not intended to do so, are in many ways a reflection of the inadequacy of current policies and practices in preparing and supporting assistant principals for their roles and responsibilities. There is much that can be done prior to role entry to facilitate the assistant principal's transition, and there is as well much that can be done to support a successful transition once it is undertaken.

While it is impossible to offer any single recipe about how to navigate the pathways along which newly appointed assistant principal's travel, the observations and insights captured by Professor Armstrong will provide newly appointed assistant principals, or teachers thinking of undertaking this leadership pathway, with many helpful ideas about the personal and professional challenges they will face, and about the critical adaptations and changes in perspective that accompany this role passage. Her research adds substantially to our understanding of the experience of the novice assistant principal, and I am confident that readers will find these pages engaging and useful, as well as mentally stimulating!

William D. Greenfield, Jr.
Professor Emeritus
Portland State University

Preface

Our careers play a central role in the ebb and flow of individual and organizational lives. They define who we are, how we live, where we work, who we interact with, and how we interpret our world and our place in it. Within the educational landscape becoming an administrator is generally configured as a logical career pathway and a rewarding experience. Every year, thousands of teachers sign up for administrator preparation programs and apply for administrative positions. Indeed, it is not unusual for new teacher candidates to declare that they would like to become administrators, even before they are in the classroom. Yet, how much do we really know about the challenges that educators experience and the social and emotional straits they encounter as they negotiate the passage from teaching to administration?

Administrative transitions are subjective and objective events which provoke personal and professional changes. In spite of its deceptive smoothness, the move from teacher to administrator is often accompanied by feelings of loss, conflict, and confusion, as novices adapt to external role demands and a different professional culture. In the current educational climate where accountability, quick turnarounds, and measurable results are the prevailing currencies, new administrators are pressured to deliver immediate results and instantaneous adaptation to new and emerging circumstances is expected. Often obscured by the rush of external demands, their leadership transitions are treated as one-time events and newcomers are typically left to navigate their administrative passages on their own.

Although new administrators are socialized to project an image of competence and calmness, these experiences resonate deeply at the social and emotional levels. They also impact newcomers' leadership pathways and practices in imperceptible ways and they carry important implications for individual and organizational success. Understanding how new administrators navigate these internal and external shifts is important for new and aspiring leaders who want to make a positive difference. This knowledge is also critical to leadership preparation programs and school districts that are committed to leadership development that matters.

Book Overview

This book examines two areas which are core to effective leadership, but are often ignored in theory and practice – assistant principals and their administrative passages. Assistant principals are vital to school success. As frontline administrators, they represent the face of school administration, and they comprise a large (often the largest) group of administrators in many school districts. Assistant principals fulfil a complex range of leadership and managerial roles in their daily work. They are also the people who community members are most likely to appeal to when in need of help, resources, and advice.

While research on the principalship and leadership preparation has increased over the past two decades, there is a dearth of studies regarding the socio-emotional nature of leadership transitions and how new assistant principals become effective leaders. For the most part, studies have concentrated on established leaders and external behaviors and outcomes, i.e., what leaders do, rather than the internal leadership landscape – how leaders think and feel (Ackerman & Maislin-Ostrowski, Armstrong, 2005). Furthermore, because this research traditionally has focused on principals and superintendents, assistant principals and their critical management and leadership roles have seldom been studied (Armstrong, 2004b; Calebrese, Kwan & Walker, 2008). Assistant principals are rarely (if ever) mentioned in leadership preparation curricula or policy documents. There are also few textbooks which focus on the social and emotional realities of this particular role transition, the changes that accompany it, and how they can be facilitated. As a result, new assistant principals and their school districts are seldom prepared for the depth and breadth of this administrative passage and its challenges for those in the process of transition. School districts as well are affected directly, because it is frequently their assistant principals upon whom they depend for maintaining organizational stability and effective relations with students, parents, and teachers.

As the base of the organizational pyramid and a key entry and socialization checkpoint for upper management careers, the assistant principalship is often the place where new administrators develop the attitudes, skills, and behaviors that shape the future direction of district leadership practices. In their role as intermediaries among students, staff, and communities, assistant principals are often asked to make difficult choices on a daily basis (Marshall & Hooley, 2006). How newcomers resolve transitional challenges has significant long-term consequences for individual careers, students' lives, and a school's organizational success. As administrative pools diminish and accountability demands increase, there is a pressing need to learn more about this administrative passage and the ways in which individuals and organizations can make this transition successful for all concerned.

Book Focus and Content

This book describes the passage from teaching to administration through the eyes of newly appointed secondary school assistant principals. While specific differences exist in the experience of assistant principals in elementary and secondary settings, much of the research, stories, and passages shared in this book will resonate with, and be of value to understanding the experiences of new assistant principals in general. The metaphor of "passages" is used to mark the progression from teaching to administration over time and space. "Passages" is also used to describe the stories that new assistant principals tell as they navigate uncharted administrative territory and create new meanings for themselves. Each assistant principal provides a vivid and unique account of his/her personal trajectory. These narratives are aggregated and contextualized to reflect the existing literature on change, transition, and administrator socialization. A visual metaphor of cycles within cycles (epicycles) is used to describe the iterative and nonlinear nature of this trajectory and the significant tensions, dilemmas, and milestones that characterize each phase of the administrative passage.

Readers will find this book engaging for a number of reasons. The assistant principals' narratives bring a personal perspective to educational administration and the process of becoming an assistant principal. The assistant principals come to administration from different walks of life, at different ages, and from a variety of ethnic backgrounds, and their stories capture the rich diversity and humanness of new administrators' lived experiences. Their narratives open up a new window on the inner and outer world of school organizations, as these men and women bridge the worlds of teaching and administration.

The assistant principals' stories uncover a hidden landscape of paradoxes and emotions which shape administrators' work lives. At the same time, these descriptions reveal a corresponding sociopolitical landscape of boundaries, rites, and rituals which operate beneath an external veneer of order, control, and stability. They also illustrate the ways in which new administrators negotiate pitfalls and politics within a shifting organizational context. As the new assistant principals describe their hopes, disappointments, and accomplishments they connect us to the complexities of change and transition and the moral imperatives of schooling.

This book offers a perspective on administrative practice which is not normally discussed in traditional textbooks. It will be of interest to practitioners, policy makers, and theoreticians alike. Professors of educational leadership and administration will find it to be a helpful resource as a primary or supplemental course text because of its theoretical and field-based relevance. Aspiring and practicing administrators can use the assistant principals' stories as a tool for reflection and discussion, and as a point of reference in mentoring prospective candidates. District and university pre- and in-service professional development programs will find the recommendations useful in enhancing their preparation, mentoring, and induction programs. Practicing administrators will see their experiences reflected in the assistant principals' stories, while administrative candidates can use this information to identify and clarify their goals as well as the types and levels of support they will need as they undertake this leadership passage.

Book Structure and Organization

This book is organized into three sections. While it is recommended that the book be read in its entirety, readers may choose the areas that best meet their professional needs. Part I (Chapters 1 and 2) provides the rationale for studying assistant principals' transitions, the background of the study on which this book is based, and its theoretical underpinnings. Chapter 1 provides a general overview of issues related to assistant principals, their career transitions, and the research study questions that guided this study. Chapter 2 reviews key psychological and sociological conceptions of passages, transitions, and socialization from the fields of career development and educational administration that inform our theoretical and empirical understanding of administrative passages and transitions. Common socialization stages, tactics, and outcomes are discussed with reference to new assistant principals' role construction, and questions are raised regarding the impact of organizational socialization on newcomers' development of leadership praxis. This chapter also highlights the importance of a person-centric approach to research that honors assistant principals' experiences and views organizations through subjective, as well as objective, lenses. It concludes with a description of the conceptual framework that emerged out of this body of research and my ongoing research on the assistant principalship.

Part II (Chapters 3, 4, 5, 6, 7, and 8) introduces new learning to the field by first sharing the individual and collective experiences of eight recently appointed secondary school assistant principals, the factors and processes that bring coherence and meaning to their journey, and providing a new model for understanding these experiences. This section of the book describes the reasons these individuals became assistant principals, their pre-role preparation and learning, and the early strategies they use to navigate the social and emotional terrain of school administration. Chapter 3 profiles the individual assistant principals' stories. The assistant principals describe their reasons for choosing this route, their preparation for the journey, their challenges, and their future vision. Chapter 4 explores the assistant principals' trajectories in further depth, and it charts the psychological and social dimensions of the administrative passage from the assistant principals' perspective. A metaphor of epicycles (cycles within cycles) is introduced to illustrate the iterative nature or the assistant principals' internal and external trajectories.

Chapters 5, 6, 7, and 8 describe the peculiar challenges and dilemmas that the assistant principals encounter at each cycle of the passage, and the strategies they use to resolve them. Chapter 5 focuses on the *Entry-Exit* epicycle when the novice assistant principals first come to the personal, professional, and organizational crossroads between teaching and administration. Chapter 6 explores the second epicycle of *Immersion-Emersion*, where assistant principals come face to face with school and district socialization impacts. This period of shocks, surprises, and "absurd contrasts" is exacerbated by the assistant principals' ambiguous location at the center of their school community. It details their efforts to make sense of the paradoxes of leadership and management and to come to terms with these role tensions. Chapter 7 explores the challenges inherent in the third epicycle of *Disintegration-Reintegration*. The assistant principals describe how they let go of, hold onto and reframe aspects of their former teacher identities and relationships, and develop perspectives that are more consistent with their new organizational role.

Chapter 8 focuses on the final epicycle, *Transformation-Restabilization*, where the assistant principals are fully incorporated into the administrative and school culture. The assistant principals discuss how they build the cognitive and emotional capacity to deal with the ongoing challenges of leadership and management and how they negotiate their administrative identity. Using images and metaphors derived from the assistant principals' narratives, this chapter discusses their overall assessment of the transition, their accomplishments, and their future career objectives.

Part III (Chapter 9) draws the book to conclusion. It calls for sustainable structures and practices which can scaffold novice administrators' developmental needs. This chapter also discusses the importance of reconceptualizing the roles of assistant principals and leadership transitions. It calls for a deeper understanding of the personal, professional, and organizational aspects of this leadership passage, and it recommends ways in which preparation and regulatory bodies can support equitable and democratic leadership practices. Finally, suggestions are provided for aspiring and new assistant principals regarding how they can support themselves and each other during this transition.

Acknowledgments

Writing a book is like a passage. It is a journey of exploration which opens up multiple pathways, and it is facilitated by the help of caring individuals. I am grateful to the many people who have supported me in the process of writing this book. Above all, I acknowledge the following people who went out of their way to ensure that this dream became a possibility. My sincerest thanks to:

Professor William D. Greenfield for his learned guidance, discerning questions, and dedication to this project;

Professor Brenda J. McMahon for her insightful critique, thoughtful challenges, and ongoing encouragement;

Lawrence Henry, Snezana Ratkovic and *Dorothy Buchanan* for their enthusiastic support, feedback, and careful editing;

Professor Paul Begley for his ongoing support and mentorship;

Dean James Heap for his financial support of Faculty of Education scholarly initiatives;

My children, *Anne-Marie* and *John*, and my husband, *Tom*, for their patience and understanding;

Finally, above all, I owe a debt of gratitude to the *assistant principals* who volunteered their time and shared their experiences with me. Thanks for trusting me with the gift of your stories.

Contents

List of Figures

Part I
Background

Passage, *pas'ij*,

Noun 1. (a) *the act of passing*: movement from one place to another; migration; (b) change or progress from one process or condition to another; transition; (c) the enactment of a law by a legislative body; 2. (a) *permission, right, or a chance to pass; journey; voyage; the accommodations of a passenger*; (b) the charge for such accommodations; 3. (a) *a way or means of passing: a road or path*; (b) a channel; (c) a hall or corridor that is an entrance or exit; passageway; 4. (a) *that which happens or takes place between persons*; interchange, as of blows or words; 5. (a) *a short segment of a written work or speech.*
Intransitive verb: to make a passage, or voyage; journey.

The *Merriam-Webster Online Dictionary* provides multiple definitions of the word passage that capture the complexities of the transition of teaching to administration. This section introduces the reader to the metaphor of passages as it relates to newcomers and their organizations, and it provides the rationale for and the theoretical underpinnings of this book. Chapter 1 situates the topic of administrative passages within the study of educational administration. It discusses why it is important to understand new assistant principals' transitions and their stories. Issues related to assistant principals, the factors and processes that shape their career transitions, and the questions that guide this work are also discussed.

Chapter 2 situates this discussion within psychological and sociological theories of change and transition that inform our understanding of administrative passages. Common socialization stages, tactics, and outcomes are discussed with reference to new assistant principals' transitions, and questions are raised regarding the impact of socialization approaches on newcomers' development of leadership praxis. This chapter concludes with a description of the conceptual framework that emerges out of these bodies of research and my ongoing research on the assistant principalship.

Chapter 1
Introduction

*The learning curve is steep. It's like 100% straight up and if you
don't have people around you to support you, your whole ego is
going to be affected. And you are going to have self-doubts
about whether you can do this job or not because you are
putting out fires on a daily basis. And then there is the transition
in your personal life. That can be quite stressful because you
have developed habits in your professional career and then, at
the beginning of September, you have to start making these
changes. You have to carry yourself as a leader in the school.
You must do the right things. You must model the right things,
and sometimes that changes your personality and your whole
demeanor changes. It has become quite stressful. You are
constantly battling smoke and fire, and you have almost literally
no time to do any personal stuff, whether it is to go to the
bathroom or have lunch. As a transition stage, you might be
lucky if you can have a period of calm before you hit the water.
You jump in off the deep end right away and you better know
how to swim.*

(Richard,[1] a new assistant principal)

Abstract This chapter situates the topic of administrative passages within the research and practice of educational administration, and it provides a general overview of issues related to assistant principals, their career transitions, and the frameworks and questions that motivate and guide this work. It discusses the paradoxical nature of assistant principals' transitions and their impact on newcomers, their school communities, and the administrative profession. This chapter also highlights the importance of developing a perspective which honors assistant principals' narratives, and allows for a simultaneous analysis of the internal and external dynamics of change and transition process.

The promotion from teaching to administration represents a significant milestone within the personal and professional landscape of education. Although it is often

---

[1] Pseudonyms are used in order to protect the assistant principals' anonymity.

seen as a logical career pathway to upper level management positions, it carries
different meanings for individuals and their organizations. At the organizational
level, this transition represents the official stamp of approval that permits access
to the inner workings of the administrator reference group and signals an elevation
within the professional hierarchy. The teacher's leadership skills have been recognized, increased professional status has been granted, and access to the corridors
of power and influence is imminent. At the personal level, it is often an exciting
period which marks the successful culmination of years of teaching and preparation. A personal ambition has been accomplished, cherished dreams have been ful-
filled, hard work and loyalty have been rewarded, and a promising future is on the
horizon.

Although the transition from teaching to administration often appears to outsiders to be a straightforward change in roles and responsibilities, new assistant
principals, including those you will meet in this book, tell a different story. They
describe a complex psychological passage that extends beyond a change in physical
locations and duties. Crossing the boundary between teaching and administration
precipitates a challenging cognitive, emotional, and social journey across uncharted
personal, professional, and organizational territory. New assistant principals, like
Richard above, are likely to find that becoming an administrator is characterized by
many shocks and surprises (Hartzell, 1991; Marshall & Hooley, 2006). Each stage
of the transition trajectory presents its own peculiar dilemmas and challenges and
requires new ways of thinking, communicating, behaving, emoting, and seeing the
educational world and one's place in it. It also entails relinquishing familiar teaching
roles and relationships that were central to their identities, adopting the core beliefs
and values of the administrative reference group, and assuming a new organizational
perspective (Armstrong, 2004b; Greenfield, 1985a). Novice administrators are often
surprised to discover the complexity of this passage and its impact on their personal
and professional circumstances (Sigford, 1998). For most assistant principals, it is
an emotional journey of self-discovery that challenges the mind, body, and spirit.

Understanding Administrative Passages

Although new assistant principals often feel alone as they navigate the administrative passage, their transitions are not isolated phenomena. Unlike teacher transitions which generally unfold within the privacy of their classrooms, administrative transitions are more public events because they occur within a larger system arena among multiple stakeholders. New assistant principals' transitions are
also deeply embedded within the larger sociopolitical context of the particular
school and district culture, and the demands of that professional role (Marshall,
1992a, 1992b). Each of these overlapping layers presents its own idiosyncratic challenges to new assistant principals, and their impacts are felt more sharply when
they co-occur within the environments of rapid organizational upheaval and professional instability that characterize many contemporary schools and districts.
These layers also increase the complexity of assistant principals' roles and their

relationships with educational stakeholders (Armstrong, 2005; Hoyle & Wallace, 2005).

Reviews of the literature show that today's new assistant principals are also likely to enter a fragmented educational landscape that is fraught with contradiction (Marshall & Hooley, 2006; Olson, 2000; Sigford, 1998). These ambiguities and their unintended consequences are highlighted in analyses of large scale British, US, and Canadian reforms (e.g., Armstrong, in press-a; Gillborn & Ladson-Billings, 2004). In many jurisdictions, parallel and sometimes contradictory reforms in curriculum, governance, and staffing which purport to simplify school management, give site-level administrators greater freedom, and improve schooling, have often resulted in tighter central office controls and produced contrary effects that impact communities negatively (Bush, 2003; Hoyle &Wallace, 2006; Leithwood, Fullan, & Watson, 2003). Assistant principals' workloads and the transitional stressors for new assistant principals have substantially increased because of overlapping professional and organizational changes related to:

- Large-scale government reforms related to centralization, site-based management, standardization, and testing (Earl, Freeman, Lasky, Sutherland, & Torrance, 2002);
- School district consolidations, downsizing, and cutbacks in senior administrative staff, with concurrent increases in legal responsibilities and accountability (Armstrong, 2005; Nanavati & McCulloch, 2003);
- Policy changes that exacerbate traditional tensions between administrators and teachers, e.g., the legislated removal of administrators from teachers' unions and administrators' legal obligation to implement unpopular reforms and compliance measures (Griffith, 2001);
- Union and district contracts and policies that create artificial distinctions between instruction and management duties (Armstrong, in press-b; Griffith, 2001);
- Changing social and economic climates and shifting population demographics (Marshall & Hooley, 2006; Williams, 2001);
- A prevailing ethic of efficiency and uniformity that ignores the unique characteristics of diverse populations and further limit educational opportunities (Gillborn & Youdell, 2000; McMahon & Armstrong, 2006).

In addition to the socioeconomic, political, and cultural factors outlined above, new assistant principals encounter idiosyncratic role dynamics which introduce additional ambiguity, further complicating their transition. A large part of the adjustment challenges that new assistant principals experience can be directly traced to the fact that the assistant principalship role lacks clear professional boundaries and policy definitions. Assistant principals who come from a teaching environment structured by clearly defined tasks and relationships and the predictability of a prescribed timetable are generally unprepared for the amorphous nature of their new administrative role and the variety of conflicting expectations and tasks that surround it.

Newcomers experience the assistant principalship as mentally and physically challenging, and many have difficulty adjusting to the hectic pace and fragmented duties that characterize this role (Hartzell, 1991; Marshall, 1985b, 1992a). Their middle management status also positions them physically, socially, and politically at the front line of the school, where they are more publicly visible and accountable to the whole community (Marshall & Hooley, 2006; Scoggins & Bishop, 1993). In most cases, they are expected to assume immediate responsibility and to make policy, curricular, and operational decisions without systematic job training, support, and mentoring.

Even if they are adequately trained to perform the technical tasks of administration, novices are often unprepared for the socio-emotional and political realities of middle management, and the challenges of their new school and district (Marshall, 1992a; Sigford, 1998). These challenges are further exacerbated for administrators who work in diverse environments because of their legal obligation to implement system policies and procedures that frequently equate sameness with equity, while striving to be responsibly responsive to changing school demographics (Armstrong & McMahon, 2006; Ryan, 2003). New administrators experience ambiguity and stress when their actions and values conflict and when they lack the power, skills, and resources to resolve the tensions and paradoxes inherent in their role (Begley, 1999, 2003; Marshall & Hooley, 2006). These professional and organizational factors impact assistant principals' mental and physical well-being, their job commitment, and their general role performance (Schmidt, Komski, & Pollack, 1998a, 1998b). When combined, they increase the complexity of assistant principals' role transitions, making it more difficult for newcomers to make sense of their experiences and to construct effective leadership practices (Armstrong, 2005).

Understanding Individual and Organizational Narratives

A growing number of theorists propose that there is consistency across human experience and stories are integral to our way of being, becoming, and experiencing. Rodriguez (2002) observes, "We are indeed narrative beings. We negotiate the world and our humanity through narratives. Narratives allow us to grapple with the ambiguity, diversity, mystery, and discontinuity that come with being in the world" (p. 3). Over the years, anthropologists, sociologists, and psychologists have used stories and narratives to explore, analyze, and interpret the cultural and emotional dimensions of individuals and their organizations, and as a means of facilitating change (Fineman, Sims, & Gabriel, 2005). In their analysis of organizational culture, Clegg, Kornberger, and Pitsis (2005) highlight three types of narratives that permeate educational environments:

- *Stories*, i.e., narratives that have their basis in true events and may combine truth and fiction;
- *Legends*, i.e., stories that are often retold with some fictional elaboration;
- *Myths*, i.e., stories that communicate beliefs which cannot be demonstrated by facts.

Organizations use all three types of narratives to manage meaning, communicate core organizational values, and to negotiate social order and identities (Clegg et al., 2005; Fineman et al., 2005). Critical scholars such as Thomas King (2003) and Bill Foster (2004) identify these master narratives as creating "truths" that reinforce hegemonic practices, while denying individual and group realities. As such, they are not neutral. As reflections of dominant ideologies and power interests, they act as normative forces to structure and direct educational research, theory, and practice (Armstrong, 2004a; Crow & Grogan, 2005; Foster, 2004). They are also part of the contested terrain of the administrative landscape and they help to maintain and reproduce existing norms and behaviors.

Educational narratives are often about school heroes or heroines who epitomize desired traits, and they generally highlight values such as courage and perseverance in the face of adversity and crisis (Clegg et al., 2005). Principals and teachers are likely to be cast in the lead roles as saviors, often defying insurmountable odds to save the day. Assistant principals (on the rare occasions they are featured) are portrayed as antiheroes, e.g., bad cops, hatchet men, and/or fire fighters, although they fulfil a wide range of instructional leadership and personnel management roles that are integral to daily school operations (Kwan & Walker, 2008; Olson, 2000; Simpson, 2000). These different narratives perform an important role in maintaining organizational and professional cultures, and they send subtle messages about what is valued (and what is not). They communicate professional boundaries, expectations, and stereotypes, and they also have a powerful influence (intentionally and unintentionally) in socializing new assistant principals.

Over the past decade, researchers have used narrative as a methodology to examine the ways in which teachers construct professional practice and identities (Clandinin & Connelly, 1994, 2006; Kincheloe, 2003). This research identifies teachers' narratives as important because they allow them to:

- Express their thoughts, emotions, and beliefs (Clandinin & Connelly, 1994);
- Describe their perceptions of external organizational realities (Fineman et al., 2005);
- Negotiate new environments and construct new realities (Rodriguez, 2002);
- Make sense of their professional experiences (Cole & Knowles, 2000);
- Construct new professional identities (Meijers, 2002; Radnor, 2001);
- Facilitate understanding of self and others as they communicate (Young & Collin, 1992);
- Remind us of our humanness and connect people across differences of class, gender, and race (Cooper, 2002).

To date, the majority of educational research has focused on teachers and principals, and assistant principals' stories still remain largely untold. There are a number of compelling reasons why assistant principals' stories should be explored. Assistant principals represent a considerable part of the administrative workforce. Assistant principals' individual and collective narratives illustrate the tensions between personal and organizational constructions of reality, providing a valuable counterpoint to prevailing organizational myths that surround this administrative role. These stories can enrich our understanding of the ways in which administrators at different levels of the organizational hierarchy navigate and interpret their roles. When considered in conjunction with teachers' and principals' stories, assistant principals' narratives can enable us to create a more comprehensive picture of the educational landscape.

Listening to Assistant Principals' Narratives

Clandinin and Connelly (1994) assert that "stories are the closest we can come to experience as we and others tell of our experience. A story has a sense of being full, of coming out of a personal and social history" (p. 415). This book is based on new assistant principals' stories of their lived experiences of the transition from teaching to administration. My interest in understanding assistant principals' role transition experiences began in my teaching career. Like most of my colleagues, I entered teaching with the stereotype of assistant principals as "bad cops," whose primary role was to assist me with difficult students. I was often critical of their decisions, and many times I felt that I could do a better job. A different perspective of assistant principals emerged in my subsequent role as a Head of Student Services. Working closely with assistant principals in supporting vulnerable students, I was surprised by the diversity of roles and approaches they used. As I observed assistant principals in action and listened to their stories, I became more intrigued with this role. Many times I wondered "What are the real stories that lie underneath their onstage, public 'presentation of self'?" (Goffmann, 1959) and "Why would anyone want to be an assistant principal?"

Becoming an administrator myself provided me with a different perspective on assistant principals' stories. I am not sure that I did a better job than the assistant principals with whom I worked with previously as a teacher. However, as I listened to my senior colleagues I became more fascinated by the stories they told and the ways in which they differed from teachers' stories. For the most part, these "war stories" were related to interactions with staff, students, and parents, and they were charged with exciting details about crises, close calls, and narrow escapes. They contained warnings about political intrigues, plots, counterplots and, in many ways, they portrayed administration as an act of improvization, or as a former assistant principal described it, "an absurd tragic-comedy often based on gut reactions, a hope, and a prayer." As a new assistant principal, these stories were critical in helping me to fill gaps in my experience. I became more aware of the norms and boundaries of administrative practice. I also began to recognize where I fit in (or in some cases, did not fit in) with my new professional community.

Working in conjunction with new assistant principals in my capacity as a principal, and as an assistant principal mentor within our local and district administrator associations, I became aware that there were some differences in the stories that novices and veterans told. The veterans' stories were often humorous, delivered with a great deal of bravado, and were often used to show how they triumphed over the system. On the other hand, the newcomers' tales were more tentative. They were used to reflect on their role, to make sense of their emerging identities, and to confirm their perceptions of the administrative landscape. Although many of their accounts were different from my experiences, I began to recognize that these stories allowed new assistant principals to bring consistency and coherence to their work, to communicate identity and practice, and to create a sense of connection with the larger administrative group.

Listening to assistant principals' stories has taught me a great deal about organizational and professional cultures, and administration as a human endeavor. As a professor of administration and leadership, my earlier interest in assistant principals' lived experiences continues to drive my research. As I listen to my students and research participants tell their stories, I recognize that these narratives:

- Help newcomers come to terms with the disjunction between their incoming expectations and the reality of this administrative role;
- Describe the diversity and similarity of administrators' lived and felt realities;
- Uncover a hidden world of emotion;
- Go to the core of the ethical dilemmas that keep new assistant principals up at night;
- Map the social, cognitive, and emotional terrain of administration;
- Reveal the tacit and articulated assumptions and values of the administrative group;
- Trace the developmental nature of administrative knowledge and behavior over time;
- Illuminate fault lines and shared interpretations between teaching and administration;
- Identify the myths, legends, rites, and rituals that circumscribe administrative behavior and school culture.

New assistant principals' narratives allow them to theorize their experiences and practices, and they act as important bridges between their teaching and administrative roles and identities. As they undergo this role transition, their stories help them to structure experience and to make sense of the discontinuities between teaching and administration. By expressing their thoughts and feelings, newcomers are able to communicate a sense of direction and of forward and upward progression, to make sense of their organizational environments, and to connect the dots between leadership theory and the daily practices of administration.

Researching Assistant Principals' Stories

The assistant principals' stories in this book are derived from my work with assistant principals as a researcher, mentor, and administrator. My approach to the study of assistant principals' experiences and their stories is influenced by the theories of phenomenology and social constructivism. These theories describe and interpret lived experiences and the ways in which people construct their world and their place in it (Radnor, 2001). Studying personal experience and narratives allows researchers to gain valuable insights into the complex dimensions of human behavior in naturalistic settings and to generate data which is "rich in the subjectivity of actions, interactions, emotions, culture, symbols and rituals" (Morgan & Drury, 2003, p. 5).

Narrative methodology is useful in showing how individuals make meaning of their experiences and construct identities. Meijers (2002) notes that people develop personality narratives which "are *interpretations* of concepts as they exist in the culturally constructed worlds in which the person participates" (p. 156). Young and Collin (1992) identify an intricate connection between narratives and personal experience:

> To make sense of the self in context and to be able to express that sense to others, the individual constructs a narrative in which events are connected to one another in relation to self and to others within a structure that integrates the parts into a whole and gives coherence and direction through time. (p. 9)

Schwandt (2000) also points out that narrative and identity construction occur as a result of a dialectical, historical, and sociocultural process and within the context of shared language, meanings, and practices. In other words, individuals construct concepts, models, and schemes in order to interpret their experiences, and they test and modify these constructions based on new experiences.

Clandinin and Connelly's (1994) use of personal experience methods shows how researchers can enter into, and participate in, personal and professional worlds and create a "middle ground where there is a conversation among people with different life experiences" (p. 425). They indicate that listening to participants' stories can be particularly useful because narratives can focus inward and outward as well as backward and forward. *Inward* refers to feelings, hopes, aesthetic reactions, and moral dispositions, while *outward* refers to external conditions of reality and the environment. *Backward* and *forward* refer to the past, present, and future (Clandinin & Connelly, 1994).

The core data upon which the bulk of the stories in this book are based were derived from an in-depth qualitative study that explored the personal, professional, and organizational transitions of eight new secondary school assistant principals. This study used qualitative[2] research methods to understand, describe, and articulate new assistant-principals' personal and social constructions of their "lived experiences" as they made the transition from teaching to administration. Qualitative research is widely used in the field of education because of its ability to deal with complexities of multiple, socially constructed realities (Radnor, 2001). It offers a

---

[2] Qualitative research is "an umbrella term" for a wide variety of philosophical orientations that support an interpretive research. Within this paradigm, reality is socially constructed and in a constant state of evolution (Glesne & Peshkin, 1992).

strong methodological framework for understanding the subjective dynamics that occur within the professional practice of educators because it provides access to the individuals' lived reality, their internal constructions, and their personal worldviews (Morgan & Drury, 2003). Description and interpretation were used to throw light on the everyday theories that inform assistant principals' behavior and experiences and to provide an understanding of thoughts, emotions, actions, and contexts.

The eight assistant principals were selected from a large Canadian province, using purposive sampling procedures (Merriam, 1998). The following four key selection criteria were used to maximize the diversity of assistant principals' experiences, biographical factors, and school contexts: (a) years of experience as a secondary school assistant principal; (b) gender; (c) racial/ethnocultural identification; and (d) type of school – vocational, mixed (vocational/academic), and academic. The assistant principals participated in face-to-face focused interviews over a 4-year period. Gathering data over an extended time period provided opportunities to establish a more solid relationship of trust with the participants (Merriam, 1998) and allowed for a richer and more developmental view of the assistant principals' transition. Each interview lasted approximately 40–90 minutes and questions were focused on:

- The nature of the transition from teaching to administration;
- The significant people, structures, and events that facilitated or hindered their transitional passage;
- The challenges and dilemmas they encountered;
- The strategies that they used to negotiate the challenges they encountered.

Because some of the data were retrospective, different types of interview techniques such as active listening and reflective questioning and feedback were used to cross-check the reliability of the participants' responses (Radnor, 2001). The assistant principals were encouraged to discuss issues that resonated with them. They also freely volunteered information related to experiences that they thought might be helpful in understanding their transition that occurred during the period that had elapsed between interviews.

Field notes were written at the end of each interview as a means of reconstructing and reflecting critically on the experience of gathering the data. Observations related to the interview context, the participants' reactions, participant and interviewer interactions, emerging responses and my perceptions and reactions were also recorded. Additional member checks entailed a built-in process of transcript review and editing by the participants. The assistant principals were encouraged to review their transcripts for accuracy and to submit additional information that might further elucidate their experience, and they were contacted by phone and by e-mail to discuss any changes that they wanted to make. Additional checks for validity included taking the data and tentative interpretations back to the assistant principals to find out if the results were reflective of their experiences.

Two interrelated but different levels of analysis and reporting were used to balance the tension of telling the assistant principals' personal stories and communicating categories that were common across their total group experiences. After the data related to the individual experience of transition were physically sorted, all of the transcripts were reread as a whole in order to determine shared tendencies and recurring patterns. Data were categorized and clustered into themes based on frequency of occurrence or nonoccurrence. Earlier discrete categories derived from the raw data of the individual interviews were compared, contrasted, and aggregated to create a composite picture of the transitional phenomena.

Developing categories of meaning allowed me to establish a closer connection with each assistant principal's personal narrative, to preserve the integrity of his or her experiences, and to communicate its essence. This process allowed for a more refined stage of conceptual categorization which involved identifying and grouping related phenomena under the personal, professional, and organizational categories described in the research framework and research questions. Part of this inductive analysis included identifying and connecting recurring patterns, critical events, themes, relationships, and narrative threads that captured the assistant principals' reports of their transition experiences. This emerging set of categories was cross-tabulated with the individual responses to determine consistencies, inconsistencies, and response patterns.

The data were then classified according to the primary research questions as well as under most frequently occurring themes. They were coded under categories generated by the researcher and focused on the personal, professional, and organizational experiences of the transition. These were further categorized under internal and external processes that contributed to the transition, including emotions, cognitions, and responses; supports, hindrances, and socialization influences; levels of preparation and support; challenges, tensions, and coping strategies; and transitional outcomes. The final stages of this analysis involved interpreting and translating the data into a conceptual framework, connecting the transitional phenomena with existing theory and literature, and communicating an account of the research that approximated the new assistant principals' experiences as closely as possible.

Researching people's experiences and telling their stories is a moral act imbued with tremendous personal and social responsibility and power. When individuals trust us to tell their stories, we owe them a duty of care and responsibility and must take into account how our stories will impact on their lives (Clandinin & Connelly, 1994; Cole & Knowles, 2000). Assistant principals' narratives embody the conflicted nature of educational leadership and they add color, depth, breadth, and texture to the educational topography. As such, they provide a framework for practitioners and theorists to develop a more comprehensive perspective of the educational landscape and to bridge teaching and administrative thought and action. When newcomers tell their stories, it creates space for them to connect the threads between their former teaching and emerging administrative identities, to make sense of the ambiguities of context and practice, and to articulate their struggles. It also allows them to reflect on and reformulate their thinking and actions and to create viable leadership pathways. These stories of resistance, compliance, and triumph illustrate the developmental nature of administrative praxis, and the challenges and possibilities that are inherent in this transition.

Chapter 2
Perspectives on Change, Transitions, and Passages

Abstract This chapter highlights key aspects of the literature on change, transitions, and passages that can inform our understanding of the passage from teaching to administration. It presents a brief overview of psychological and sociological theories of transitions and passages, and it draws parallels between commonly identified transition and socialization stages, processes, and outcomes and their impact on new assistant principals' administrative passages. This chapter concludes with a discussion of the conceptual framework that guides the analysis of the personal, professional, and organizational dynamics of the assistant principal's administrative passage.

There is general agreement among psychological and sociological theorists that change is fundamental to the growth and survival of human and social systems. It is also not uncommon to find metaphors such as *passages* (Glaser & Strauss, 1971; Sheehy, 2006; Van Gennep, 1960), *journeys* (Bridges, 1980), and *trajectories* (Nicholson & West, 1989) to describe how people move between personal and organizational roles and identities, and across time and space. However, while theorists may converge in their language and the belief that change is important, qualitative differences exist in the ways in which they view the interface between people and institutions. For the most part, traditional psychological frameworks highlight the subjective or internal nature of change. They ask: How do individuals create their own organizational realities? On the other hand, sociological theories focus on the external and objective aspects of this passage. They ask: How are people formed by their organizations? The following sections provide a brief overview of the key characteristics of psychological and sociological perspectives on change.

Psychological Perspectives – Transitions as Personal Change

Psychologically based theories focus on the personal and subjective nature of change and the ways in which individuals adapt to change on the affective, cognitive, and behavioral levels. Models of change and transition tend to be grounded in theories of human life-span development and grief and crisis counseling, which describe how people adjust to major life stressors (e.g., marriage, divorce, and career change),[1] and for the most part, theorists establish an interactive relationship between change and transition. In other words, "change leads to transition and transition leads to change" (Viney, 1980, p. 16).

Although the terms change and transition are sometimes used interchangeably, Bridges (2001) argues for a clearer distinction between understandings of change and transition. He locates transitions within change and contends that although they are often used synonymously, change is a situational shift, while transition is the process of letting go of the way things used to be and taking hold of the way they have become. Change is the outer force, while transitions are the internal psychological processes that individuals go through as they cope with change. Bridges (2001) asserts:

> Without transition, a change is mechanical, superficial, empty. If transition does not occur or if it is begun or aborted, people end up (mentally and emotionally) back where they started, and the change doesn't work. (p. 3)

The following characteristics appear consistently in descriptions of transitions:

- They are generally conceived as "events or non-events" or processes in the individual's life (Brammer, 1991; Bridges, 2001, 2003);
- They are triggered by external or internal change events or personal dynamics in the individual's life (Abrego & Brammer, 1992);
- They signal strains and stresses in an individual's life (Abrego & Brammer, 1992; Nicholson, 1990);
- They elicit responses that are ambivalent, whether they are voluntary or involuntary (Marris, 1974);
- They may be experienced as negative or positive depending on the individual's capacity to utilize appropriate coping and adjustment strategies (Bridges, 2001);
- They enable individuals to make fundamental changes in their worldview;
- They motivate corresponding changes in relationships, roles, responsibilities, and/or behavior (Hopson & Adams, 1976; Viney, 1980);
- They provide opportunities for psychological growth or deterioration (Adams, 1976; Schlossberg, 1981).

Transitions precipitate a series of fairly predictable phases or cycles which build on, or flow into, each other and they lead to a new phase of development (Brammer, 1991; Bridges, 2001). They usually follow a three-phase or stage pattern which includes a *precipitating change event*, a *middle state*, and a *new beginning* (see, for example, Bridges, 2001, 2003; Lewin, 1947; Viney, 1980). The first stage occurs when a *precipitating change event*, such as a promotion to administration,

---

[1] Studies confirm that positive career events such as promotions can precipitate a sense of loss as the individual discards old roles, identities, statuses, and locations and adopts new ones (Abrego & Brammer, 1992; Hopson & Adams, 1976; Sigford, 1998).

precipitates cognitive, emotional, and behavioral responses, marking the onset of the transition.

According to Bridges (1980, 2001), during the *middle state* or neutral zone, the transitioner attempts to make sense of his or her new world. Because transitions provide experiences that contradict existing assumptions, they create a state of disequilibrium or a feeling of "betwixt and between" the old world and the new one. Unexpected feelings of loss pervade this intermediary stage because the individual's identity is enmeshed with his/her life circumstances, roles, and relationships. The individual may experience disengagement (separation from what is lost), disidentification (loss of the old identity), disenchantment (moving out of the old reality), and disorientation (feelings of loss and bewilderment that occur as a result of losing the old identity). The experience of disequilibrium and loss leads to the final stage of *new beginning*. The individual develops a new perspective and is able to integrate the transition into his or her own life. He or she develops new relationships and values and focuses on new goals and aspirations.

Social Perspectives: Transitions as Social Passages

Transitions may also be described as a sequence of passages which outline paths that mark turning points when social personas change and identities are in flux (Hagestad, 1991). The notion of transitions as social "passages" has its origins in Van Gennep's (1960) anthropological research on life transitions in traditional societies and the movement of individuals from one position in a social structure to another (Butler, 1998). Van Gennep (1960) describes three stages, *separation, transition*, and *reincorporation*, whose structure closely parallels the psychological models which were described in the previous section.

During the first stage of *separation*, the individual is isolated from his or her familiar social context. This is followed by *transition* or a *liminal* stage, which is characterized by a period of isolation where newcomers are in an "ambiguous state of 'betwixt-and-between'" (Trice & Morand, 1989, p. 400). During this middle period, individuals are subjected to a "grinding down process" (Brown, 1995; Van Gennep, 1960) where they face ordeals, impossible tasks, humiliations, and tests. These rites provide the receiving group with an opportunity to evaluate the desirability and worthiness of the newcomer. They also overlap with a verbal and non-verbal rebuilding process where newcomers are exposed to new skills and learn the secrets of the group (Brown, 1995; Trice & Morand, 1989). During the final stage, *reincorporation*, initiates are reintroduced to the society or a smaller group. Having successfully completed the specified rites and rituals and demonstrated their worthiness and ability to fulfil the expectations of the new position, they are accorded commensurate rights and obligations, and are expected to behave according to the customary norms and ethical standards of their social position (Cobb, 2005; Wollon & Sommer, 2003).

Glaser and Strauss (1971) use the concept of "status passages" to describe how individuals integrate socially and adapt to work. They describe careers as a series of passages from one role to another within an organizational or occupational social system, and they identify three stages – *status*, *transitional status*, and *status*. Like psychological transitions, status passages have multiple dimensions and have the following characteristics:

- They are interpreted and responded to depending on individual characteristics and the dimensions of the passage;
- Individuals can go through more than one passage concurrently;
- They may be scheduled or unscheduled;
- They may be voluntary or involuntary;
- They may be perceived as desirable or undesirable;
- They can be of high importance to the person going through the passage or unimportant;
- They may or may not be subject to the person's control;
- Their duration may vary.

While the rites and rituals of passage required to gain administrative status appear to be less stringent in modern societies, they tend to fulfil the same functions. They facilitate social and psychological movement between roles, and they also involve the manipulation of symbols and the use of scripted behaviors (Ashforth, 2001; Cobb, 2005). Brown (1995) observes that most forms of probationary status in our culture place newcomers in a liminal or transitional relationship with the group to which they seek membership. Trice and Beyer (1984) and Trice and Morand (1989) establish close parallels between organizational socialization practices and Van Gennep's (1960) analysis of rites of passage in traditional societies. They describe rites of passage, degradation, integration, and enhancement as common in today's organizations. These rites encourage the development of a role identity, build group cohesion, and affirm organizational values, beliefs, and ideologies. The following section discusses additional aspects of role transitions and socialization that further illuminate our understanding of assistant principals' transitions.

The Assistant Principalship – Career Transitions and Socialization

Career theorists acknowledge the interrelationship between the individual and his or her context, and they integrate sociological and psychological constructs in order to explain how organizational newcomers adapt to or are motivated to adapt to professional and/or organizational role changes. Louis (1981) defines a career transition as "a state and a period during which an individual is either changing roles (taking on a different objective role) or changing orientation to a role already held (altering a subjective state)" (p. 57). The promotion from teaching to the assistant principalship is consistent with Louis' description of an inter-role transition because it entails assuming a substantively different objective role. Inter-role transitions require a passage across organizational boundaries, and they extend from the entry period until the individual reaches substantial adjustment to, and acceptance of, the role. Individuals undergoing inter-role transitions are faced with several tasks such as adjusting to the reality of the organizational context, learning how to work, dealing with the boss and the reward system, and developing an identity and place for himself or herself in the organization (Louis, 1981). Because subjective inter-role transitions tend to happen concurrently with objective transitions such as promotions, they may not be as easily perceived by new assistant principals.

To date, the area of career transitions has been subject to very little empirical research. Consistent with the general trends in the field of organizational studies, researchers and theorists tend to focus primarily on the effects of external organizational socialization, as opposed to how individuals change from within (Ashforth, 2001; Saks & Ashforth, 1997). The educational administration literature also mirrors these trends. For the most part, these studies focus on the socialization of principals, and it is not uncommon for authors to generalize these findings to the assistant principalship. This information can be misleading, and it may create confusion for new and aspiring assistant principals. Even though principals and assistant principals engage in similar duties, their socialization impacts differ because of their relative status in the administrative hierarchy and the different types of power and privilege that are vested in these two roles. As subordinates to the principal and as front line middle managers, assistant principals are subject to different socialization influences. The following sections highlight studies that examine how newcomers adapt to administrative transitions, with specific reference to factors and processes that mediate the move from teaching to administration.

Transition and Socialization

Organizational socialization has been the dominant theme in the literature, and there seems to be a general agreement that it functions to transmit and perpetuate organizational culture and stability (Greenfield, 1985a; Major, 2000; Saks & Ashforth, 1997, 2000). Definitions of socialization vary depending on the theorists' perspective of the relative influence of the individual and the organization on this change process. Within traditional schools of thought, newcomers such as assistant principals are seen as playing a passive role and are at the mercy of organizational forces (Saks & Ashforth, 1997). This worldview has been challenged by interactionists, who contextualize the internal psychological process of change and transition within the social environment. Bullogh, Knowles, and Crow (1991) assert that meanings emerge from the social interaction between people. This view argues that socialization is better described as "an active process of world building rather than a passive adaptation – after the manner of functionalism – to an institutionally defined role and patterns of relations" (Bullogh et al., 1991, p. 6).

The administrative socialization research identifies two main types of socialization, i.e., professional and organizational (Hart, 1991; Matthews & Crow, 2003). Professional socialization is the process of becoming a member of a profession and identifying with its norms and beliefs. Although the point at which professional socialization starts has been subject to some debate, it is generally hypothesized to begin when the teacher begins to consider administration as a career (Hart, 1991; Michel, 1996), to interact with other administrators, and to internalize the behaviors, knowledge, skills, and dispositions needed for professional membership (Hart, 1991). This includes formal training by school districts and universities, and informal socialization experiences that help shape administrative candidates' notions of what it means to be an administrator (Greenfield, 1985a; Marshall, 1985a; Matthews & Crow, 2003).

Alvy and Robbins (1998) define organizational socialization as the transition period from the time the individual is appointed as an administrator until he or she is accepted in the organization. Organizational socialization is the process of learning the knowledge and skills associated with one's role and setting, and it modifies, reinforces, and expands the generic skills and attitudes learned during university training (Heck, 1995; Matthews & Crow, 2003). Greenfield (1985a) further categorizes organizational socialization into technical and moral aspects. Technical dimensions include the acquiring and use of appropriate role-related skills, knowledge, and techniques. Moral dimensions relate to adopting and internalizing group values, norms, and attitudes and are central to gaining acceptance into the administrative group.

Although organizational and professional socialization play important roles in assistant principals' transitions, organizational socialization overpowers professional socialization if the two conflict (Marshall, 1985a, 1985b). This may be attributed to the fact that supervisors determine promotions and other job-related rewards, while colleagues control social interactions (Hart, 1991). Gold and Douvan (1997) also point out that newcomers are more likely to be susceptible to influence during role transitions because they are uncertain of their roles. In addition, newcomers are more likely to effect organizational change indirectly through their impact on culture.

Transition and Socialization Stages

For the most part, new administrators' socialization stages are modeled on the business management theory and research (see, for example, Nicholson, 1990; Nicholson & West, 1988, 1989; Louis, 1980, 1981). These theorists use stage frameworks to describe the progression from novice to experienced practitioner, to explain how individuals think and act, and to support growth and development (Goodman, 2001). Stages have their own distinct qualities and require mastery of specific developmental tasks (Abrego & Brammer, 1992; O'Connor & Wolfe, 1991). However, because each individual's transition is unique, stages do not necessarily occur in fixed and progressive steps or in a smooth, continuous pattern; they may blend into each other, overlap, and repeat in a continuous process (Brammer, 1991; Bridges, 2001, 2003). Each stage of socialization presents different challenges, and newcomers are likely to encounter a wide range of different organizational tactics from different educational stakeholders (Matthews & Crow, 2003).

The research on organizational socialization suggests four broad stages of *anticipatory socialization*; *encounter*; *adjustment*; and *stabilization*.

Anticipatory socialization: Atchley describes anticipatory socialization as "the process of learning the rights, obligations, resources and outlook of a position or situation one will occupy in the future" (as cited in Schlossberg, 1981, p. 2). This first stage of pre-arrival and preparation occurs prior to the new administrator's placement in the school when he or she is learning about the assistant principalship and rehearsing for the role. Hart (1993) locates it at the period when the individual has been selected as an administrator and has made the decision to leave his or her position to take the new role, while Greenfield (1985a) and Matthews and Crow (2003) identify it as beginning even earlier, when teachers start thinking about pursuing the administrative track. Anticipatory socialization is an important part of professional and role socialization since the individual is acquiring information about their targeted role and how it is viewed by the larger society, universities, and mentors (Hart, 1993; Matthews & Crow, 2003). Merton's (1968; in Greenfield, 1985b) concept of anticipatory socialization suggests that the transition begins with a positive orientation to the possibility of taking on a new role. Administrative candidates and professional development providers can do a great job during this pre-entry period to facilitate entry, transition, and role adjustment.

Encounter: The second stage of Encounter begins when the new assistant principal assumes the role and is confronted with the technical, social, cognitive, and emotional tasks of administration (Hartzell, 1991; Hartzell, Williams, & Nelson, 1994; Marshall, 1985a, 1985b). This early contact period can initially be experienced as a period of excitement because of the new work content and context (Brammer, 1991; Nicholson & West, 1988; Sigford, 1998). However, it is more likely to be characterized by shocks and surprises, and negative surprises tend to be the most common experience for new administrators (Greenfield, 1985b). The degree and kinds of shocks and surprises that new assistant principals encounter are a function of their psychological readiness, technical preparation, school setting, and conflicts between their personal expectations and values and institutional norms (Marshall, 1993; Marshall & Mitchell, 1991). New assistant principals generally discover that the anticipations they developed during teaching and/or their administrative internship conflict with the reality of the school environment. This is further compounded by the fact that community expectations of assistant principals tend to vary by school setting and culture, and novices are faced with the stress of deciding which interpretation to use (Marshall & Hooley, 2006).

Adjustment: Fitting in and becoming an insider are critical tasks of the Adjustment stage. The newcomer's ability to adjust is influenced by individual, organizational, and social factors such as personality characteristics, levels of support such as mentors and supervisors, job characteristics, and group dynamics (Nicholson &

West, 1988, 1989). Hart (1993) describes this as the period when new administrators reach accommodation within the culture of their new school and their administrative work role. Administrators at this stage develop a more realistic sense of their role and the ability to deal with its ambiguities. They also demonstrate improved management and interpersonal skills, increased commitment to the organization, and altered or reaffirmed self-images and values (Hart, 1993; Marshall, 1985a, 1992a; Matthews & Crow, 2003).

Stabilization: The final stage of Stabilization occurs when newcomers are socially and psychologically located within the organizational context. It is a period of role management and stabilization where administrators are engaged in internal and external negotiations with members of the school environment (Hart, 1993). Their behaviors become more congruent with organizational and role norms, and they attempt to demonstrate personal and organizational effectiveness (Ashforth & Saks, 1996). This is also likely to be the stage where assistant principals may be inclined to apply for the principalship.

Other models also exist. For example, Sigford's (1998) study of new principals and assistant principals is noteworthy in its departure from traditional organizational socialization paradigms. Her emphasis on the socio-emotional dimension of change provides a more holistic perspective on transitions by refocusing attention on the personal and relational nature of administrative passages. Using Kubler-Ross' five stages of grief – *denial, anger, bargaining, depression*, and *acceptance* – as a framework for understanding the change process that occurs as a result of the loss of the teacher role and identity, Sigford proposes that adapting to a major personal change, like a job promotion, is a nonlinear process which is typified by "uneven ups and downs" (p. 13) and may last for approximately 2 years.

Denial: The first stage is initially accompanied by positive feelings because of the role's novelty and status. The denial of the first stage comes from the novelty of the position, the office, and the tasks, and it is initially experienced as euphoria because of the status that is accorded to the role. New administrators still think they are teachers although they may feel some emotional distance from staff. They also experience a sense of loss because they are leaving a known identity and peer group. The main task of denial is to help newcomers separate from their old role and redefine and integrate their previous learning into the new position.

Anger: The second stage occurs when new administrators' and teachers' opinions differ. Anger surfaces as a result of these conflicts, and it may be accompanied by the blaming of others. New administrators often use anger as a way of masking the fear and sadness that they feel.

Bargaining: During the third stage of bargaining, new administrators start bridging teaching and administrative experiences, developing coping strategies and finding ways to improve their situation. The fusion of denial and anger allows new administrators to refocus on the future and to look for ways to do a better job. These strategies are part of the external remedies needed to build a new internal self-definition and may include attempts to learn new management skills and support faculty.

Depression: This stage typically occurs near the end of the second year, and it may be masked by frustration, exhaustion, stress, or self-doubt. New administrators question their choice and consider other career options. Depression may be temporary, but it is necessary for the final letting go that facilitates growth.

Acceptance: This final stage occurs around the third year when newcomers realize that they cannot go back to teaching. It is often evidenced in feelings of self-assurance about their accomplishments.

Transitions and Socialization Impacts and Mediators

The ability of new administrators to adapt to role changes is dependent on a variety of personal, sociohistorical, and environmental issues. Although these factors interact dynamically to influence transitions, they can be loosely categorized under three broad sets of independent variables which include (1) the characteristics of the transition; (2) the characteristics of pre- and post-transition environments; and (3) the individual characteristics (Abrego & Brammer, 1992; Dotlich, Noel, & Walker, 2004; Viney, 1980).

Transitional Characteristics: Adjustment to transitions is influenced by the type of role change. Important factors are similarities between their prior role and the assistant principalship; positive or negative feelings about the change; timing and intensity of the change and whether it conflicts with other life changes; and whether it occurs gradually or suddenly.

Characteristics of Pre- and Post-transition Environments: Contextual factors also play an important role. These include professional preparation, training, and development for the assistant principal's role; interpersonal support networks such as family and friends; the principal's leadership style; administrative team relationships; institutional sponsors, mentors, supports, and resources, as well as induction practices; hidden and articulated role expectations and requirements, assigned duties, tasks, and responsibilities; type of school and physical setting; and school district culture and climate (Armstrong, 2005; Greenfield, 1985a, Hartzell et al., 1994; Marshall, 1992a; Marshall & Hooley, 2006; Matthews & Crow, 2003).

Individual Characteristics: The ability to adapt also depends on personality and background factors. These include gender and sex role identification; age and life stage; race and ethnicity; socio-economic status; physical and psychological health; related administrative experiences; attitudes and values; interpersonal and intrapersonal competencies; and coping abilities (Hartzell et al., 1994; Matthews & Crow, 2003; Spector & Fox, 2002).

Transitions and Socialization Tasks, Tactics, and Outcomes

In spite of the fact that transitions and socialization play an integral role in shaping behaviors and outcomes, socialization often occurs by default (Ashforth, 2001). Socialization tactics may also vary between and among institutions, and different cultures and stakeholder groups impose different demands on new assistant principals (Marshall, 1985a; Matthews & Crow, 2003). For the most part, educational stakeholders are unaware of the methods they use to socialize newcomers and are not aware of how they impact new administrators (Hart, 1991; Marshall, 1985a). However, whether conscious or unconscious, organizational socialization practices regulate assistant principals' transitions, and they define a number of technical, moral, and political tasks that novices are required to master in order to be accepted within the school culture.

The following competencies appear consistently in the literature on new assistant principals' transitions, socialization, and acculturation (Armstrong, 2005; Hartzell et al., 1994; Marshall, 1992a; Marshall & Mitchell, 1991):

- Performing their assigned duties;
- Learning the local language and culture;
- Defining their role and territory;
- Learning the rules and limits of their role and organization;
- Earning their supervisors' recognition and trust;
- Understanding how and when organizational power can be used;
- Building a role identity and locating themselves in the organizational culture;
- Developing relationships within and outside of their immediate work group;
- Managing between and within group tensions;
- Balancing the conflict between work and personal life.

Different socialization methods produce different results. Furthermore, individual and group outcomes are difficult to predict because each assistant principal brings his or her own perspective and expectations to the role. While some maintain the status quo, others encourage change and innovation.

Role Taking, Making, and Innovation

Reviews of the literature on administrative socialization found that the three most commonly predicted outcomes of socialization are content innovation, role innovation, and replication. Role taking and role making are the two main forms of socialization and are critical to constructing new roles (Hart, 1993). Role taking is a form of replication which occurs when new assistant principals enact their assigned administrative script in a custodial manner. It is evident in cases where new administrators conform to past practices and accept the prevailing organizational and professional norms and beliefs without question (Greenfield, 1985a; Hart, 1991; Matthews & Crow, 2003). This form of role taking preserves and perpetuates the dominant professional and organizational status quo which limits newcomers' agency and their ability to construct viable leadership roles, and to change the school culture (Greenfield, 1985c; Sigford, 1998).

In contrast, role making highlights the interpersonal and active nature of role construction and it "shifts emphasis from the simple process of enacting a prescribed role to devising a performance on the basis of an imputed other role" (Fein, 1990, p. 14). While new assistant principals may accept traditional scripts, they may also use other tactics and tasks, and may draw from a knowledge base that is unconventional (Matthews & Crow, 2003). Role making coheres with Greenfield's (1985a, 1985b) description of role and content innovation. Content innovation occurs when new assistant principals make modifications to their role and attempt to substantially improve or change role practices, tactics, or tasks while still accepting its traditional values (Greenfield, 1985a, 1985b; Matthews & Crow, 2003). Role innovation is the more radical response to organizational socialization. It occurs when newcomers attempt to actively mold the job to fit their own values, expectations, and perspectives (Hart, 1993; Matthews & Crow, 2003). This may involve attempts to redefine the purposes and practices of a role, to make changes to its goals and content, and to reject most of the traditional strategies, and norms of administration (Greenfield, 1985c; Hart, 1991).

Given the current emphasis on school leadership, reform, and improvement, one would think that administrative socialization would lead to innovative role orientations and leadership practices which can facilitate positive organizational changes. Unfortunately, custodial responses are the most commonly reported socialization outcomes for school administrators. Although content and role innovation are possible, they are seldom evident in schools (Armstrong, 2005; Greenfield, 1985c; Hart, 1991; Heck, 1995).

The literature highlights pervasive institutional, individual, and role dynamics that prevent assistant principals' adoption of innovative roles. Greenfield (1985a) identifies a gestalt of socialization tactics that ensure conformity and role replication. New assistant principal socialization tends to be individual, informal, random, variable and serial, and involve investiture and divestiture processes (Van Maanen & Schein, 1979). This combination of tactics ensures that maintenance of the organizational status quo is the most likely outcome. At the same time newcomers' anxiety is increased, and they are more likely to shed their former teacher values and loyalties and to adopt the prevailing orientations of the administrative group.

At the role level, assistant principals are socialized to be boundary spanners and buffers between the school and the external community, bridging a variety of competing roles and stakeholder interests, dealing with ongoing safety threats, and protecting the technical core of the school. Assistant principals' maintenance, stabilizing, and disciplinary functions directly contradict innovative or transformative responses. Matthews and Crow (2003) also connect the assistant principals' subordinate role in the administrative hierarchy to their inability to create innovative leadership roles. Assistant principals are often constrained by their principal's leadership style and top-down approaches, and novice assistant principals receive clear signals that they must buy into the system, learn the rules, and emulate their administrative superiors in order to get ahead. These structures are further reinforced by mentors and veteran staff who put pressure on new assistant principals to maintain pre-established norms.

Marshall and Greenfield's (1987) analysis of assistant principals' enculturation identifies intolerance of ambiguity and a strong pressure for conformity as inhibitors to role innovation and organizational change. Marshall and Mitchell's (1991) examination of the new assistant principals' assumptive worlds also uncovered powerful forces that ensure conformity by limiting the careers of assistant principals who transgress the cultural norms of administration. Marshall (1992b) also identifies district hiring and promotion practices as factors that ensure custodial practices. She indicates that assistant principals are not only selected because of their conservative outlook, but they are further socialized to avoid ambiguity and risk taking. Assistant principals who critique the status quo are unlikely to be trusted by their more powerful peers and are likely to be sanctioned. New assistant principals also receive clear signals that, in order to be successful in the organization, they must buy into the system, obey the rules, and follow existing practices and procedures (Marshall, 1992b).

It is clear that the kinds of socialization practices new assistant principals encounter have a formidable impact on their transitional passages and the leadership pathways they choose. Adopting the custodial role orientation restricts new assistant principals' agency and inhibits their ability to introduce reforms or to change existing approaches to their role. Since most assistant principals enter this role with a desire to improve schools, key questions which must be asked are: How can assistant principals navigate these socialization challenges and evolve a more innovative role orientation? How can educational institutions create structures and processes that support the development of transformative leadership praxis?

Matthews and Crow's (2003) notion of socialization as a reciprocal process, where both new administrators and their schools actively engage in professional learning, presents a more constructivist vision of socialization that has the potential to lead to positive change. Within this paradigm, the new assistant principal and his/her school negotiate role taking and role making. Matthews and Crow (2003) also urge new assistant principals to adopt an attitude of "creative individualism" which involves the acceptance of pivotal values and norms and rejection of the others.

The preceding discussion highlights the different ways in which theorists conceptualize change transitions and passages. It shows that, for the most part, new administrators' transitions are seen through organizational socialization lenses. The following section proposes an interactive framework which allows us to examine the passage from teaching to administration from the personal perspective of new assistant principals.

Adopting a Person-Centric Perspective on Transitions

This book uses a person-centric approach to the study of transitions. This perspective is consistent with change theories that emphasize the importance of individual agency and the social and emotional dimensions of transitional passages from the perspective of the person in transition. This vantage point allows theorists and practitioners to map out newcomers' passage across social boundaries as well as the organizational structures that facilitate and constrain their choices and shape their values and behaviors (Nicholson & West, 1989). Looking at the administrative passage through the eyes of newly appointed assistant principals provides a different perspective on the administrative landscape. It opens up an important window for examining and uncovering established norms and beliefs and taken-for-granted practices. It also shows how individuals are influenced by professional and organizational factors and how they resist and/or reproduce existing practices.

A person-centric perspective on organizations is also used to integrate the psychological and social aspects of role transitions and to provide simultaneous analyses of the subjective and objective aspects of new assistant principals' administrative passage. The model that I use to interpret administrative passages and transitions (as discussed briefly in Chapter 1) is derived from my work with assistant principals as a researcher, mentor, and administrator. It is based on the premise that people and careers change and develop over time through the interaction of a variety of individual and environmental factors (Abrego & Brammer, 1992; Ashforth, 2001).

My interpretation of the assistant principals' experiences is also influenced by career and leadership theories which stress the dynamic interrelationship between social, political, economic, and cultural variables, and considers how societal norms and organizational design impact individuals' choices and leadership constructions (Cooper, 2002; Lambert, 2002). It is also shaped by the belief that leadership is a moral and reciprocal process which can be organized and enacted in ways that facilitate human development, encourage educational growth, and engage communities in the construction of shared meanings and purposes (Walker, 2002). This focus departs from traditional approaches which examine role transitions through the external lens of organizational socialization, and it is important for the following reasons:

- It integrates and bridges the duality between traditional psychological and sociological traditions;
- It maps the socio-emotional terrain between teaching and administration;
- It provides a deeper understanding of the internal and external evolutionary processes that newcomers experience as they leave teaching;
- It allows us to understand what happens "inside the head," i.e., how professionals think and what they value (Gardner, Csikszentmihalyi, & Damon, 2001).

As such, this perspective enriches and extends the prevailing focus on organizational socialization because it allows us to explore assistant principals' stories of their lived experiences and to answer questions that can inform and improve individual and organizational practice, such as: What social and emotional factors impact administrators' trajectories? What are the turning points in their careers? Why do they pursue certain pathways? How and why do they resist or conform to organiza-

ADMINISTRATION PASSAGE

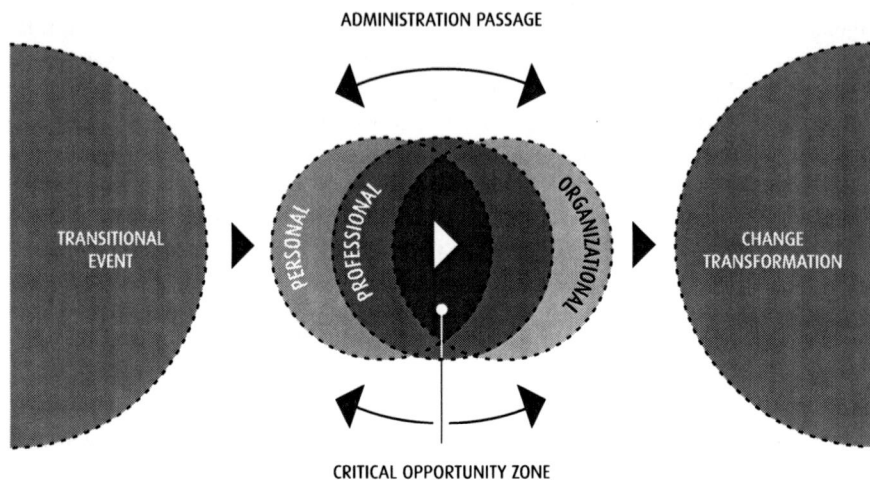

CRITICAL OPPORTUNITY ZONE

Fig. 2.1 The passage from teaching to administration

tional pressures? What is the impact of this adjustment on the person in transition? How are administrative and teaching identities formed or transformed?

Administrative transitions represent a complex dynamic which occurs as a result of the interplay between personal, professional, and organizational phenomena. Figure 2.1 depicts the passage from teaching to administration and the various factors which impact the new assistant principals' transition. Transitions and passages often begin with a precipitating event (Abrego & Brammer, 1992). In this case, the decision to pursue an administrative career (far left of the diagram) triggers the onset of this transition and propels the individual into the administrative landscape. This marks the beginning of the administrative journey, and the newcomer enters the administrative passage.

The overlapping circles that are located in the middle of Fig. 2.1 depict the embedded nature of the assistant principal's personal, professional, and organizational spheres. The dotted circles and arrows are used to depict the cyclical and open nature of this dynamic. The outcome depicted on the right side of Fig. 2.1 represents the result of the transition. It is hypothesized that personal and professional change will occur as a result of this passage.

The *personal* circle comprises the assistant principal's intrapersonal and interpersonal domains. This includes psychosocial factors related to the assistant principal's attitudes, emotions, cognitions, skills, values, motivations, expectations, background and personality variables, as well as their relationships with family, friends, and community. The *professional* circle includes mediating factors which define their membership within teaching and administration. It comprises their administrative and teacher colleagues, professional associations, written and unwritten codes of behavior, norms, traditions, and the theories-in-action which guide discursive practice. The *organizational* circle constitutes micro and macro structures, events, and processes within the internal and external school community and the surrounding political context that impact the assistant principal's work life.

The shaded area at the centre of the diagram marks the intersections of these three arenas. This represents the critical "opportunity zone" in the assistant principal's role transition, and it will be the primary focus of the remainder of this book. The disequilibrium that occurs as a result of these intersecting domains generates a dynamic which destabilizes the individual's psychological and social worlds, and stimulates growth and transformation. This premise is also consistent with theories that highlight the "crisis" and "opportunity"[2] value of transitions (Adams, Hayes, & Hopson, 1976; Bridges, 2003). Transitions provide an opportunity for psychological growth as well as a danger of psychological deterioration (Hopson & Adams, 1976; Schlossberg, 1981). Crises in this sense are not catastrophes. Rather, they should be seen as turning points, where an individual has increased vulnerability and a heightened sense of potential (Sheehy, 2006).

The "opportunity value" (Adams et al., 1976, p. 2) inherent in this transitional zone is important for both individuals and organizations because of its creative potential and its possibilities for renewal and transformation (Adams et al., 1976; Brammer, 1981, 1991; Hopson & Adams, 1976). The nature of the role change and transformation process is dependent on the skills, dispositions, and characteristics of each assistant principal, as well as the opportunities and spaces that are created by their organizations to support their leadership growth.

Using constructs derived from my previous and current research and the sociological and psychological literature (Abrego & Brammer, 1992; Nicholson, 1990; Nicholson & West, 1989; Schlossberg, 1981), I propose that it is within this opportunity zone that novice assistant principals negotiate and construct administrative identities and leadership praxis. This is a dynamic socio-emotional process which is scaffolded by their internal thoughts and feelings, and is reinforced by their interactions with the external environment. This notion is constructivist in nature, and it is an extension of Vygotsky's zone of proximal development, i.e., the field among learners and teachers where meaning, knowledge, and intelligence are mediated (as cited in Lambert, 2002). Leadership construction is therefore not a fixed commodity. Rather, it is an evolving process which exists in the relationships that occur between individuals and their communities (Lambert, 2002). The outcome of this role change and transformation process is dependent on the skills, dispositions, and characteristics of each assistant principal and the opportunities and spaces that are created by their organization to support their leadership growth.

This conception of new assistant principals' passages is grounded in my belief in the transformative and developmental nature of administrative leadership (Armstrong 2004a, 2004b). Assistant principals' leadership is therefore not a predetermined commodity or necessarily vested in their title. It exists in the relationships and processes that occur among individuals and groups. This perspective is

---

[2] According to Adams (1976), the Chinese word for "crisis" comprises the merger of the words "danger" and "opportunity" (p. 157).

consistent with paradigms of constructivist[3] leadership (Lambert, 2002; Walker, 2002) that propose that learning occurs through a process of knowledge construction, inquiry, participation and reflection, and that possibilities for learning and leading permeate and inform actions, interactions, and community spaces within the school culture (Cooper, 2002; Lambert, 2002; Walker, 2002). It is hypothesized that personal as well as professional change and transformation occur as a result of this passage. The following chapter introduces the eight new assistant principals and highlights key aspects of their personal journey.

---

[3] Constructivism is a theory of learning and knowing that draws primarily from the fields of philosophy, psychology, and science and is based on epistemological concepts derived from the work of Dewey, Piaget, Bruner, Vygotsky, Feurestin, and Kegan (Walker, 2002).

Part II
Narrating the Administrative Passage

*The gift of personal presence is to be able to tell the
stories of our others*
(Glesne & Peshkin, 1992, p. 8.)

This section focuses on the individual and collective stories of the eight recently appointed secondary school assistant principals. These narratives describe the personal, professional, and organizational dimensions of the administrative passage and the early strategies the assistant principals use to map the social and emotional terrain of administration. These stories were derived from focused conversations with the assistant principals at different stages of their career passage, and they describe the motivations, dreams, and challenges which brought coherence and meaning to each individual's journey. The four women, Esther, Sandy, Barb, and Karen, and the four men, Michael, Jerry, Greg, and Andrew[1] were intentionally chosen to represent the diversity of schools, ethnicities, gender, and life stages of new assistant principals, and as a result, they do not represent the current demographics of the assistant principalship.

Chapter 3 profiles the individual assistant principals' stories. The assistant principals describe their reasons for choosing this route, their preparation for the journey, their challenges, and their future vision. Chapter 4 introduces a trajectory model which describes and charts the psychological and social dimensions of the administrative passage from the assistant principals' perspective. Chapters 5, 6, 7, and 8 describe the paradoxes and dilemmas that the assistant principals encounter at each cycle of the passage, and the strategies they use to resolve them. Chapter 5 focuses on the Entry–Exit cycle when the novice assistant principals first come to the personal, professional, and organizational crossroads between teaching and administration.

Chapter 6 describes the second cycle of Immersion–Emersion, where the assistant principals come face to face with school and district socialization impacts and the ambiguities of their middle-management role. It details their efforts to

---

[1] These pseudonyms were chosen in order to ensure the assistant principals' anonymity.

reconcile the tensions of leadership and management and to make sense of their role. Chapter 7 explores the challenges inherent in the third cycle of Disintegration–Reintegration. The assistant principals describe how they let go of, hold onto and reframe aspects of their former teacher identities and relationships, and develop perspectives that are more consistent with their organizational role.

Chapter 8 focuses on the final cycle of Transformation–Restabilization, where the assistant principals are fully incorporated into the administrative and school culture. The assistant principals discuss how they build the cognitive and emotional capacity to deal with the ongoing challenges of leadership and management, and negotiate their administrative identity. Using images and metaphors derived from the assistant principals' narratives, this chapter discusses their overall assessment of the transition, their accomplishments, and their future career objectives.

Chapter 3
The Individual Narratives

Abstract Chapter 3 introduces the eight secondary school assistant principals. It describes their reasons for becoming assistant principals, their pre-role preparation and learning, and the factors and processes that bring coherence and meaning to their journey. While they arrived at the administrative threshold through the common route of the department headship, each individual brought different histories, philosophical orientations, and identities with them. The assistant principals are introduced according to the number of years they have been assistant principals, progressing from the most recently promoted to the most experienced. These profiles provide a personal context for their reasons for choosing an administrative pathway, their preparation for the journey, their successes and challenges, and their vision for the future.

Michael's Story

> I said to somebody that it's nice to be alive because this whole process of trying to be a vice-principal has opened a world of emotion to me. I remember Sidney Poitier and hearing him being interviewed. And he said, "Oh, it's great to be alive." You get to feel this and everything is wonderful. You feel enraged, you feel happy, you feel sad, and that's going on inside you. And this is what happened when I found out about getting the vice-principal job.

Michael and I first met during his third week as an assistant principal. As he provided a context for his school and retraced his administrative pathway, he communicated a mixture of excitement, enthusiasm, and awe about his new position, the variety of people and experiences he had encountered to date, the number of things that he had learnt, and the changes he had undergone. Michael was placed in a large suburban school of approximately 1,600 students and 100 teachers. Two thirds of the teaching staff had been there for over 20 years and the students were primarily middle-class and of European backgrounds. He described his placement as a "great school with a lot of tradition and a lot of pride in its history."

Michael depicted a complex administrative passage which was characterized by surprises, mixed emotions, and soul searching. He recalled a period of questioning which involved discussing his plans with his fiancée, parents, friends, and colleagues as he weighed the negative and positive aspects of the job. Although he was interested in becoming a school leader, he was also reluctant to become an assistant principal because of his concerns about the punitive nature of this disciplinary role and its potential negative impact on his relationship with students:

> Originally, I said to myself, "Why do you want to be a vice-principal? You have to deal with all the discipline, and you have to do all this stuff and it's not nice stuff that you have to deal with." And then I heard all these people saying, "Oh, you know, there's so much stress, you get dumped on from above, and you get dumped on from below, and why do you want to be that?"

Michael also connected his initial reservations to personal doubts about his suitability for the managerial demands of an administrative role. Having become a teacher because of his disenchantment with the politics that pervaded his former role as a supervisor, he was reluctant to leave the classroom. Furthermore, he was also proud of his accomplishments as a curriculum leader in the business department of a large school where he was respected by staff, students, and administrative colleagues:

> And I said, "You know what? I think that I am done with administration forever and ever. I just want to be a classroom teacher, not worry about being responsible for anything aside from the classroom and taking on all these initiatives and everything. Worrying about having to deal with people playing political games and everything... All of that ... done!"

Although Michael was not fully convinced that he wanted to become an assistant principal, he also believed, deep down, that an administrative role would allow him to have a greater impact on the educational system:

> So, then I got more confident that it was something that I could do. I think I can do a good job and can make a difference. And so this is my opportunity as a vice-principal to deal with all these kids and try and get them to go down the right path. So that's the difference. I still have the individual student difference that I can make.

Swayed by encouragement from his parents and his administrative colleagues and the belief that his youth would allow him time to approach the administrative pathway slowly, he decided to qualify himself by doing some of the prerequisite courses. He recalled thinking: "I'll get the paperwork done. I've got twenty years left in my career. I don't need to rush this."

Michael's decision to become an assistant principal further crystallized during a pre-certification course, where he met a group of enthusiastic administrative candidates who encouraged him to take the principal's certification courses with them. Shortly after completing his certification courses, Michael was approached by a fellow teacher and department head who encouraged him to join him in going through the district's promotion rounds. Although he was not fully committed to becoming an assistant principal, Michael decided to use this opportunity as a way to test the waters and to familiarize himself with the process:

> He said, "Michael, come on. We have to do it together. We have to support each other." I said, "Alright, I'll do it for practice." You know, as a learning experience, and then when I'm really ready, I'll do it.

As one might have anticipated, without powerful administrative sponsors and a demonstrated commitment to administration, he was unsuccessful in this first attempt. Michael, who considered himself to be "pretty level headed," was surprised by the contrasting emotions he experienced as he went through the district promotion process. He was also jolted by his reaction to the news that he was unsuccessful even though he had not fully committed to the process. He described how, feeling chastened after being rejected in his first round of interviews, he became driven to succeed:

> I was really disappointed, because now I had been working. . .I thought, "Wow, I didn't get it, and now I want it. I want it more than ever." And so, I did the whole round the second time and that went fabulously. I was humbled after my first experience and then I really did a good job at preparing. The first time it was practice. And the second time it was for real in my mind. So I did a good job of preparing and it went well and I got myself on the promotion list and the next thing you know, here I am.

Getting on "the list" was an important milestone on Michael's administrative pathway. Again, his emotional response was out of character when he received notification from his school superintendent that he was successful in the interview process:

> I found out I got on the list and I did like kind of a happy dance. And my excitement is more than normal. Normally, it's just like, "Oh, great . . . pat on my back." But this was like, "Yes! I got on the list!"

However, the euphoria of having his name placed on the list was followed by feelings of self-doubt and frustration when he discovered that, because of poor communication between superintendents, his name was omitted from the official promotion list that was published by the school district. Additional confusion was also created by his inability to get concrete information from the sending and receiving superintendent or his principal regarding his new placement:

> So one day passed, two days passed, and I hadn't got this call. So I go down to my principal and I said, "I got a call the other day from the superintendent. She said that I have been placed. Have you heard anything?" He said that he hadn't heard anything. And I am thinking to myself, "Uh oh. I don't think this is a joke, but I'll just continue to do what I've always been doing."

Reflecting on his overall administrative career trajectory, Michael described "a steep learning curve" which had been fraught with surprises. Although he had been told that his school had few disciplinary problems relative to others in his district, during his first few weeks, he had to evacuate the school because of bomb threats and a noxious chemical. He was also involved in resolving gang-related conflicts and expulsions:

> Everything has been novel, exciting and I've got a lot of support. And thankfully, the staff here is wonderful. And I have a wonderful team. They have been very supportive. People understand that I am a new kid on the block and that I am coming from teaching. It's not like I have been a vice-principal somewhere else. And so, they have been a little bit forgiving of the two or three times I have made a mistake or two.

However, in a subsequent interview, he indicated that he had experienced ongoing testing by students and parents. In addition, he indicated that the initial "honeymoon period," when he felt welcomed by staff was also over. He expressed disappointment as he recalled incidents where veteran staff had intentionally misled him by providing inaccurate or incomplete information, and/or had highlighted his lack of knowledge to his principal:

> I know a couple members on staff have taken advantage of my newness, and if I had asked a couple more questions, I might have been able to get the answer myself instead of finding out when somebody else complained. And I really resent the fact that people tried to do that because now I trust them less and it is going to take a long time.

He connected some of these negative incidents to some of his staff's comments about his youth and minority status and, as a result, he felt additional pressure "to prove himself":

> There is the piece that I am a minority. So (a) "I get the job because I am a minority." So there is pressure there. I want to make sure that, you know what? It's because I have earned the right to be here. And there's (b) "Oh, and you are so young ..."

As he compared his teaching and administrative career passages, Michael identified the latter as more difficult because of the accelerated pace of this transition, the level of responsibility, the number and variety of demands, and the lack of opportunities for apprenticeship, mentoring, and training:

> Here, there are a lot of gaps that I am filling in as I go along. Like all the systems ... systems have been the big one to get to know right now. Like staff attendance, the field trip policies, and the other specific systems we use in the school. Like all these things I am responsible for that I had to learn, whereas, with teaching, I had to learn them, but I had to learn them on my time, whereas now, I have to learn them yesterday.

In spite of his personal and professional challenges, he was determined to establish his credibility as a curriculum leader and a compassionate administrator. This commitment led to longer working days which negatively impacted his sleeping and eating habits and personal relationships. Throughout our conversations, Michael remained optimistic about his promotion and his future as an assistant principal, particularly when he compared his lot with that of other assistant principal colleagues:

> I seem to be in a very good situation. Maybe half of it is my temperament, but a good friend of mine, when he got promoted to vice-principal, he kept thinking about wanting to go back to the classroom because he didn't have any support. He felt that he was working so many hours, his health was going down, and my experience has been different.

Although he used the analogy of a tornado to capture the turbulence of his transition experiences to date, he remained pleased with his overall progress and his ability to grow as an administrator:

> So the first tornado has gone through, the big one...and I realize that I got through it. So when other situations come up, I get more comfortable dealing with them...I guess right now you just roll with the punches and I am doing my best. And I am confident that in the end, although I probably will make mistakes, in the end I'll be OK.

He attributed his confidence to a variety of direct and indirect sources of support inside and outside of the school environment, and felt that they have been important to his success. His parents have been an ongoing source of support, always willing to listen to him and encouraging him to learn from his mistakes. While his new wife was not initially comfortable with his decision to leave teaching, she had been supportive and he believed that she would eventually "come around." Michael also identified a range of supports within the administrative ranks at his present and former school and within the larger school district:

> There are people who have taught me that are still vice-principals and they also say, "If you ever need anything. . ." So, I've got a lot of people that I can draw on. So I think that I am in a very fortunate situation. And this school is a terrific school.

Michael's immediate plans were to continue "learning the ropes" and to support his community. He hoped to become a principal some day, and he believed that with time and experience he would be able to make large-scale changes that would improve schools.

Esther's Story

> I believe it is going to change. I believe that I am going to get back to my priorities and I am going to eventually get those done. But I think, in learning the job and fulfilling my role, these are things that I have to do, and they are just as important. But I think eventually, I am going to know how to manage my time and get what I need to get done. . .to have an impact and to be effective, which is why I came into it in the first place.

Esther was an assistant principal in a large, urban, multicultural school with a population of approximately 1,500 students and a faculty of approximately 115 teachers. Our conversation began during her third month on the job, and she was eager to talk about her experiences and the complexities of her administrative role. Esther was motivated to become an assistant principal because of her experiences as a teacher and parent and her desire to be a positive role model for minority students. She provided a context for her motivation:

> The students were looking for people that they could identify with. A number of people have done studies in the area and said this is the case. Students need to have a true representation of who they are in literature, in admin and in the school system. So then, I decided that I was one of those people who should get into a leadership role so that I could bring change in that area. So that's why my interest developed.

Esther believed that her professional and academic qualifications combined with her practical experiences as a curriculum leader in guidance and special education and her skill as a school and community change agent qualified her to fulfill the assistant principal's role. She also believed that her desire to learn new information and skills has been an asset in this transition process:

> I went to a lot of conferences. Anything that I felt would add to my knowledge base, I did that, and not so much because I wanted to be in this role, but because I enjoy that type of

learning. I have always done courses. So I am a lifelong learner and I think that has helped
me to prepare in the sense that my mind is always open.

After completing additional teaching qualifications in several subject areas, a
Masters program, and the principal certification courses, she applied for promotion.
Nonetheless, in spite of her background and skills, she was "passed over" for 5
years. Fearful of being targeted if she complained she remained silent. However,
after appealing to her superintendent she was finally promoted. She expressed frustration at perceived inequities within her district's promotion process:

I feel that I have a story to tell where this is concerned. Firstly, I'll start off by saying that
principals have too much power where this [promotion and hiring] is concerned and too
much control for people getting ahead, because this can be done very much on whom you
know, who knows you, and who they feel they want to support. And it has very little to do
with ability. And I found out with my own experience.

Esther reported experiencing mixed emotions when she heard the news of her promotion. As a mid-career educator, she felt that she had missed an opportunity to
make a significant difference for students because of biases that were inherent within
her district's promotion processes. She observed:

For some reason, I did not feel that excited because I felt it was long overdue. And I was
ready, and I was very ready about three years ago. And I just felt that they should have
utilized my skills before. So, to me it was like it is almost too late now that they have given
me this position. And I could have done so much. So from that perspective, I wasn't really
that excited, but I was happy to see that, yes, at least the time has come.

Esther's introduction to the assistant principalship was challenging because of
the speed of her transition and the demanding nature of the role as an urban school
assistant principal. Being promoted during the second semester was also at a disadvantage because the school year had already started and the other administrators were too busy or inexperienced to orient her to the school and her role. She
observed, "They just throw you in there, and then they say, 'Do this, do this, do
this. . .' Everything is really fast." Although she possessed a wealth of experience
with urban schools, she was surprised at the number of roadblocks she encountered
because of her lack of training and unfamiliarity with the inner workings of her
school. Reflecting on her early experiences, she observed:

For me, getting this school was not too bad because I know the neighbourhood and I have
come from a school with the same types of needs. But, what I found overwhelming was
learning the protocol. Who plays this role? Whose responsibility is this? Who are the important key players? So that was a little bit of a setback, but that didn't take me long to sort
through.

During the early months of her transition, she was also astonished to discover the
wide range of expectations and responsibilities which were attached to her administrative role. The number and type of demands which teachers made of her, in spite of
her relative lack of administrative training and experience, were also an eye-opener:

I am surprised at how much teachers look up to you, and expect you to know the job and
respond appropriately and without preparation and practice, and experience. . .that is something that new vice-principals have not been exposed to. You need that kind of training and

time or you could find yourself in deep waters. They really expect you to give the right answers and to be knowledgeable.

As an assistant principal in a large urban school, Esther encountered endemic social problems which hindered her students' learning in spite of their academic potential. She expressed discomfort about ongoing conflicts between teachers and students and the external pressures from staff to use punitive zero-tolerance approaches to resolve endemic social issues:

> Sometimes I feel that they have the wrong perspective on my role because I am really here to work with them to make life better and to encourage the students to achieve at a higher level. But sometimes they see it more as problem solving and I don't think it should be.

As she developed familiarity with her role, Esther became increasingly concerned with the reactive and punitive nature of her job and saw this focus on "grass-roots issues" as an impediment to her ability to effect positive large-scale changes. Throughout our conversations, she posed a number of questions about her true purpose as an administrator and how she could use her time and skills properly in order to create equitable conditions for students, particularly those from minority backgrounds. She observed:

> I want to do the work, and I want to be involved, but sometimes I wonder if I am fulfilling the needs of the students the way I really want, to raise the level of expectation and academic standards.

In spite of these ongoing barriers, Esther remained optimistic about her position and her ability to help others. Esther identified a strong network outside of the school. Her husband, children, and her faith congregation were supportive. Although she found it difficult to establish close personal relationships with her administrative colleagues, they had been helpful in providing information and backup support when needed. She also felt that she had a strong network of administrators and other resources that she could tap into at the district level. In addition, she had a long-standing connection with her superintendent, whom she could contact if she had a problem.

As she reflected on her early experiences and looked forward to the future, she expressed the belief that she would move beyond this phase to a different level, where she could support students, build community capacity, and work collaboratively with teachers and parents:

> I think it is a very great experience and I am hoping I will be able to impact on lives, be they parents, students, education as a whole. And I have a personal drive to go further as an educator. I have a good working relationship with others. I feel that I am going to be stronger later on in getting my point across and getting the change. I have the ability to bring people together. That's one of my strengths.

Esther continued to maintain a positive outlook about her school and her ability to achieve her goals for equity, in spite of these early challenges. She also believed that she would become more efficient over time, and she hoped to become a principal one day so that she could fully utilize her leadership skills.

Jerry's Story

> So, I know it is a political thing. I know it is a money thing. I know it's a transitional
> thing. So, on one side, I understand it. On the other side, it just becomes very draining and
> frustrating. I don't think I'm incapable of doing it, I just think that if I am doing this same
> thing two years from now, I'll walk away. So maybe, I'll get better at it. Maybe I'll get
> better at not caring.

My conversations with Jerry began during his seventh month as an assistant principal. He was placed in a large urban composite school with a population of over 90 faculty members and 1,500 hundred students. He described his student demographic as "transitory." Most of them were new to the city or the country, and they stayed in the area for approximately 1 year and then moved on. Jerry was motivated to pursue the assistant principalship because he had reached a career plateau. He had been a department head for over 5 years, he was in his forties, and he was looking for a challenge and an opportunity to help others:

> Boredom. The truth is, after you have challenge, and after you have become a department
> head for a while, you think, "Can I do this for another 20 years until I retire or should I look
> for a bigger challenge?"

Jerry prepared himself for the assistant principal's role by pursuing the principal qualification courses and his post-graduate degree, as well as a number of subject-related professional qualifications. He approached the assistant principalship pathway with confidence, based on the belief that his strong leadership record and his previous experiences in the front office of a small school would prepare him for administration:

> Being in a small staff and sort of seeing what the vice-principals did, being on committees
> and knowing that it was going to be more of a paper trail and sort of more of an organiza-
> tional position rather than a hands-on teaching position. Like, I really kind of knew what it
> was.

However, in spite of these convictions, Jerry reported that his application for promotion to the assistant principalship was rejected by his district's selection team several times, because of his principal's lack of support.

Jerry described his introduction to the assistant principalship as a harrowing experience. His initial excitement about his promotion was soon tempered by feelings of uncertainty when he realized that he would be placed in a different division of his school district which required a daily commute of at least 90 minutes. He also described several layers of adjustment related to role, task, and cultural differences. His ability to perform his role effectively was further exacerbated by a lack of systematic training for his position and district cutbacks in administrative and support staff. As he recounted these multiple challenges, he observed:

> And so, the learning curve was immense. I came here and I had to learn a whole new
> computer system. Not being a guidance person, not knowing all the codes, so that took a
> lot. Not knowing the organizational structure of the schools in this region, with curriculum
> leaders and program team leaders and trying to figure out who is who on a new staff of 100.
> Dealing with the everyday insanity of a big building, and still trying to get into classrooms
> and see teachers and make my own decisions about who's good, who's bad, who do I need

to talk to, who do I need to see to get things done. It was very tough with that other stuff on top.

Jerry's transition to administration was further complicated by a difficult school climate, which was characterized by adversarial administrator, faculty, and student relationships. Jerry attributed a large percentage of his early hardships to his principal's dictatorial management style:

> And when I first started a month in, I was ready to walk away. And that was not because the job was too hard, but my direct supervisor's philosophy and understanding of education and the way to treat kids was not mine. And it was interesting, because in my whole life, in any other job that I had done, I had never worked with a supervisor like that one.

He identified a "bunker mentality" which maintained divisions between stakeholder groups, and he experienced conflict when his principal insisted that he adopt adversarial and punitive approaches with staff, students, and the community. His early attempts to bridge relationships with staff were met with distrust and also provoked his principal's anger. She responded by prohibiting him from socializing with the teaching staff, which further increased his feelings of isolation:

> And being told things like, "I don't want you to have lunch with the staff or have coffee with the staff because it's us and them." Not allowed to sit at a staff table at a staff social.

He also described "frequent bullying tactics" which his principal used to monitor his work and control his communications with others. In addition to constantly checking his work, she would humiliate him in front of staff and students by questioning or overturning his decisions.

> And I was staying here until 8 and 9 o'clock at night, hand writing report cards, signing every report card and checking every one. Every piece of paper that went out to the staff or the parents or the students in any form, even if it was a short little memo for a meeting had to be okayed by her. No purchasing cards, no spending, no nothing. And being new coming in, being eager, coming back into a big school for me, I really got sort of lost.

Jerry experienced his principal's abrasive management style and control tactics as an ongoing source of stress and he considered complaining to senior management. However, as a new administrator without union rights, he was afraid of negative career repercussions. After considering his options and consulting with his wife, he was determined to quit his job during his first year because of concerns about his physical and psychological health and well being. However, he was disappointed to find out that he could not return to his former teaching position, and there were no central office positions available in his area of expertise.

Jerry described his second year as easier because his principal was transferred to another school. Although the overall challenges had not changed significantly, working with a principal who shared similar values of collaboration allowed him to reach out to staff to establish more viable working relationships. He also identified cultivating closer relationships with the office staff. While his interactions with the teaching staff became more collegial, he was unable to establish relationships of trust because of the existing administrator/staff divisions. However, he remained optimistic that this situation would improve over time:

They were extremely aloof and very formal. I did not form one friendship on this staff. I
still haven't. But that's OK. I think there are some really good teachers here and there is
some really good stuff going on. I like a lot of the staff.

As he reflected on his transition, Jerry described making significant progress
in terms of his knowledge about people and school systems. Over time, he was
able to work with his administrative colleagues and teaching staff to implement a
number of student leadership programs and to improve students' test scores. He
identified his ability to build relationships with students and parents as an ongoing source of satisfaction. He also saw his South Asian background as an asset,
and he was proud of his engagement in collaborative endeavors with parents and
other community members which allowed him to support immigrant and minority
students:

And this may sound weird, but being the only person of color on an administration makes a
huge difference in this community. Parents will come in and they see me and they gravitate
to speak to me. And we have so many brand new immigrants, and so I like to get out.
I want to help them, but again, it's frustrating because can't always be here until 9:00 at
night.

Although the high administrator, staff, and student turnover at his school was an
ongoing contributor to his stress levels, he pointed out that it had also increased
his commitment to poor students and his ability to adapt to changes. Having
worked with four different principals, he believed that he had learnt a great deal
about school administration and the impact of different leadership styles. However, he continued to be concerned about the reactive nature of his job and the
challenges of creating a culture of high academic achievement with limited district
support:

It's tough because it's an inner city school. It's an inner city school devastated by politics and
violence and money. Issues here are like any inner city school whether you're in Chicago,
L.A., New York, or Montreal, it doesn't matter. Unless you have a good plan and good
leadership to figure out how to solve it, you're just treading water. . . It makes my job almost
impossible to accomplish all the things. I am doing things and people say, "Yeah, we like
you, you are doing a good job", but the reality is I am doing a 50% job on most of these
issues. I can't commit. I don't have the time or the energy to really go after the things I
need to do. I spend a lot of time fire fighting in this building instead of doing curricular
changes. I spend a lot of time trying to make people feel safe and it is an effort in this
building.

Throughout our interviews Jerry remained optimistic about his tenure as an
administrator and his ability to help students. As he discussed his long-term plans,
he admitted that he had abandoned his earlier ambition to become a principal
because of district politics and negative feedback from his superintendent. However, he indicated that, in spite of its challenges, he was interested in working in his
current school until retirement. He openly expressed admiration for his students'
abilities and a commitment to working with his school district and staff to improve
his school: "I'm proud of this place and the kids are going to be proud."

Sandy's Story

> There was certainly support from my colleagues – my VP and my principal. But the other
> people, the teachers, they don't have time for this transition thing. You are in the office,
> that's your position, that's your role, these are my needs, what can you do?

When Sandy and I first met, she was in the eighth month of her first administrative placement in a large suburban multicultural school with over 1,900 students and
150 staff members. Sandy's decision to become an administrator crystallized early
in her teaching career, but she decided to "hold back" because she wanted to raise
a family. She connected her motivation to "personal, altruistic, and even political
reasons" related to her desire to advance professionally, to be a positive role model,
and to be in a position where she could improve the educational system:

> You can have positive influence at every level. But when you move on up the system, you are
> also getting closer and closer to the bigger picture to make changes. And those are changes
> that you think would benefit kids, all kids...make the system better for all of them. You
> know, I have kids too. And it's something I enjoy. So, why not be part of it? Try to make it
> better.

From a political standpoint, her locations as a parent and as a minority female were
crucial factors which she believed would allow her to address some of her concerns
about racial representation, while making structural changes from the inside:

> But also, on the political level, if I can call it that, as a minority female, you often hear about
> the lack of representation. I always ask myself, "Well, what do you do?" And I do believe
> that in order to make change you have to be in the system as opposed to be outside of it. So
> that to me is important. You can't make change without participating.

Sandy believed that demonstrating her competence through active leadership roles
in her school and achieving success in the principals' qualifications courses earned
her colleagues' respect. After being encouraged by one of her principals, she applied
for the district's promotion rounds and she was successful. She observed:

> And I think then I proved, not only to myself, but also to my peers, and certainly to my
> supervisors that I definitely had that leadership potential. So it was recognized also from
> the outside and confirmed with me.

Sandy experienced the transition to the assistant principal role as a "trial by
fire process." There was little time for orientation, information sharing, or training because she arrived at the beginning of a new semester when all of the other
administrators were busy addressing scheduling and registration matters and her
predecessor was only available to meet with her once because she had been transferred to another site. Sandy described her induction as follows:

> So I had a very brief meeting. I think we met for two hours. So that was the extent of
> my preparation. But I had lots of files in this drawer and lots of pens, and I asked a lot of
> questions and all that kind of stuff.

Sandy had always believed that she was a "person who walks through life
calmly," and she was caught off guard by the intensity of the emotional responses

she experienced as she left teaching. Her changes in physical and professional locations were accompanied by feelings of loneliness and isolation because they entailed a reduction in the size of her network of associates. Commenting on this emotional void, she admitted, "I did have to make a sort of an emotional adjustment. And one of them is that there is that sudden loss of a community of peers." The feeling of being outside of the larger group was further reinforced by us/them divisions between teaching and administrative staff:

> I think I also sensed that divide, that great divide which is much more pronounced between teachers and administration. You're really not part of the crowd. Even going into the lunchroom, you know, people are afraid. It's not that there is any animosity. You know you are different. You're not part of the inner circle and you are not always privileged to every type of conversation. I feel I'm now more part of the office instead of the staff room.

Sandy described the assistant principalship as a demanding and unpredictable role which required adjustments in terms of how she managed her time and dealt with different constituents. Unlike her former teaching position where she had a specific schedule, her administrative role was ongoing. During one of our late afternoon conversations she commented:

> In fact my lunch is in the car actually, because I didn't get a chance to eat it. But it is very easy not to take care of yourself as a VP. As a teacher, you have your lunch at 11:30 and you have your hour. As a VP, because there are no defined limits to your time, you don't have the same blocks.

She was also shocked by the fact that, in spite of her lack of training and experience, she was immediately assailed by students, parents, and staff who expected her to address problems on her own and demanded immediate solutions, "So I was certainly treated as if I was on the job for a lot longer than I was, and [the expectation was] that I should just fall in and perform. Just do it."

As time progressed and she became more comfortable with her administrative role, she observed:

> When you start, because there is so little preparation for the position, they throw you in there. The first stage is just grueling. You are watching as best you can, getting out there, getting to know things. It's certainly getting easier and I don't like it any less than I did in spite of the difficulties and frustrations.

Although Sandy described her early days on the job as difficult, she remained confident about her new position and her feelings of self-assurance were validated by comments from her colleagues:

> When I got into the job itself, I felt a lot of comfort and confidence, really. And people often said that to me that they were rather surprised. I would hear back that people had said, "Has she been a vice-principal before?" Or people would tell me their stories, you know, "By six weeks I was in tears", and I wasn't any of those things.

During her fourth year, Sandy was transferred to a vocational school. In spite of having to adapt to a different school culture, duties, and responsibilities, she observed that these experiences have not impacted her negatively in the long run. She attributed this to her positive attitude, and her ability to manage stress, and to work with people: "So I went in there knowing that I did not know anybody. But, I did have an attitude that I was going to make it a good experience, really." As she looked back on her career pathway, Sandy attributed her success as an assistant principal to her ability to use time wisely, to establish priorities, and to balance her personal and professional life. She expressed optimism about her future as an administrator and was looking forward to becoming a principal in the near future.

Greg's Story

> The honeymoon period is over. I don't think I have to prove very much to anybody. I've done most things already twice, and so it wasn't just beginner's luck...So there is that evidence there that I am not falling in that same pothole every single time. So I think people have let go of that [perception]. And that's a wonderful feeling.

Greg was an assistant principal in what he described as a suburban, middle-class, composite school of approximately 1,400 students and 80 staff where "the majority of the population is privileged, given even the city's indicators," and the students, staff and parents were "for the most part wonderful and positive." Greg connected his decision to become an assistant principal to the desire for a new challenge and saw the administrative pathway as a logical career progression from his leadership role as a teacher and curriculum leader. This internal need combined with the encouragement and support of administrators at the school and school district level provided him with the feeling that he was moving in the right direction.

Our conversations began during his second year, and during our first meeting, he spoke confidently about his preparation for his current role. Not only had he been in a curriculum leadership position where he worked closely with his previous administrative team, but he had also served informally as an assistant principal for 2 years in another school district. He believed that these experiences contributed to his familiarity with the role and provided him with opportunities for leadership that were not typically available to regular department heads. He experienced little difficulty during the early preparation and interview process, because of encouragement from his family and strong support from a network of administrators which he had developed over the years as a teacher and department head.

Although Greg was elated by his success in the district promotion process and his assignment to a school which was specifically chosen to match his strengths, he recalled a turbulent beginning, when he and the other administrators were mandated to start school earlier in order to adjust teacher timetables because of union contract changes. This feeling of chaos was further exacerbated by a district consolidation, which led to decreases in administrative and office staff and the introduction of new and unfamiliar technology and tasks. Support was lacking from his administrative team members who were also struggling to process these new initiatives, policies, and technical systems. He described a period of testing and compounding layers of stress:

So it started the year off, in this environment where there is so much change, with another layer of unpredictability. It does get resolved, but it brings an additional level of stress on everybody. So all of it was a hope and a prayer.

His feelings of insecurity were further exacerbated by pressure from staff to conform to their expectations:

So the staff already came in a little bit negative at that time and being new, they weren't sure who I was. And obviously they had to test who I was and things like that, so that was part of it.

Greg experienced the assistant principalship as a paradoxical role because of the contrasts between its vast responsibilities and its lack of power. He also resented having to do tasks, such as cafeteria supervision and data entry, which he believed could be more efficiently handled by secretaries and hall monitors. He also lamented the lack of opportunities to work directly with staff and students, and he wondered if he had made the right career move:

So the amount of time that we are in front of a terminal, I think that you could certainly use people who know and who are capable and competent to do that and to expedite matters much more quickly, rather than having a vice-principal. So I really believe that our talents and the reason why we were hired, I think that the school district and the Ministry are wasting a lot of money.

His growing sense of alienation from the job was increased when his attempts to implement changes in his new school were frustrated by school and district practices. Recognizing that he was unable to make a positive difference for students, he decided to explore other alternatives in the field of education. However, after finding out that he could not return to his former role, he decided to commit to the position. When he compared his second year experiences to those of his first year, Greg depicted an easier transition. He attributed this primarily to the fact that he was developing a supportive network as well as increased familiarity with his portfolio of responsibilities and the culture of his school:

I am feeling more comfortable this year because we didn't change our portfolios, except for adding on the work of one third of the VP that we lost. And the fact that we have a new principal who has a different leadership model...but having done this one year, I feel confident that I will be able to also deal with the other problems that will come. So, having one year under my belt provides a lot of comfort because I am repeating some things that I did before, whether it's exams, whether it's other organizational matters.

While he was able to build positive relationships with some of the staff and students he continued to be frustrated by the lack of time and structured opportunities to develop curriculum initiatives with staff. He continued to be disappointed by the reactive nature of the assistant principalship, and he mourned the loss of his ability to be a curriculum leader. Nonetheless, he was becoming more persistent in fulfilling his goal to be a curriculum leader and was more confident in integrating his strengths into the role.

For example, there are a number of areas in this school where there are opportunities for cross-curricular education. I'd love the opportunity to be able to explore those possibilities with them. So there is some experience that I think I have, that I'd love to share with staff, especially with partnerships. So I had the anticipation that I'd be able to use that history and then I'm stuck in the office most of the time. So that was disappointing.

As he reflected on his transition, Greg identified behavioral and perceptual shifts as he moved from teaching to administration. Commenting on how the demand environment of administration forced him to adopt a more conforming approach, he observed:

> I tend to question things and I need to feel that there is validation and that I trust people. So I don't take orders readily, but I also feel that as an administrator, there is duty and responsibility and organization. . . .. I've learned that I have to be more conservative and so I am coming to it with less resistance than I used to.

Having developed a better understanding of his role and its paradoxes, he expressed an increased determination to impose his own personal constructions on his role:

> The only way around it is stubbornness, because I will do it. So contact with teachers and students is critical and important. So contact with parents and teachers is critical and important. I make a point of it. For example, I organized an art exhibit for the staff so that I could bring some of that sense of collegiality and the sense that teachers are practitioners and professional. . .to value what's going on, to get into the mix of things. So I will do it by virtue of my personality.

During follow-up interviews 4 years later, Greg indicated that at this stage in his transition, he was better able to navigate the system and he was engaged in a number of leadership roles within his school and district. In addition, he had been successful in his district's interview process for principalship and had received confirmation that he would be promoted shortly.

Karen's Story

> I knew it was a bigger school. I was all excited because it was a new school with a program that matched my background. But when I found out at that time that there were over a hundred teachers and almost two thousand students, I did panic a bit. I thought, "Am I ready for this? Why did they give me such a big transition?"

Karen was an assistant principal in a large suburban school, where the majority of her students were from middle-class backgrounds and the parents and teachers focused primarily on high academic achievement. Our conversations began in her third year and she described her experience as "extremes in more than one sense." Her former school was a small, collaborative special education school which focused on teaching individual students life skills. At her new school, the student population was twenty times larger, the teachers were polarized into their subject departments, and teacher–administrative relationships were at a low. Karen was initially reluctant to apply for an assistant principalship because she enjoyed her role as the Head of the Guidance Department. However, after the administrative team in her school convinced her that she had the prerequisite skills and experience to fulfil the demands of the assistant principalship, she overcame her misgivings and decided to do the required qualifications. She recalled an earlier conversation with her principal:

> He sort of said to me one day, "You know what? You are doing what an administrator is doing already. So why not go ahead and get your papers and go for a position, because you have the experience".

Karen described a chaotic beginning to her journey as an assistant principal. Her initial excitement at having been informed by her superintendent that she had been placed on her district's promotion list was soon replaced by feelings of insecurity when her name was omitted from the published list. When her attempts to receive concrete written proof were rebuffed by a superintendent, she questioned whether she was ready for this move. Karen's introduction to her new school was unsettling because of the number of cognitive, social, and emotional adjustments she had to make. She was overwhelmed by the physical and cultural differences between her current and former school and she missed the collegial interactions between the administration and the teachers. She observed:

> I'd been a couple of times and I'd always found it, I don't know if it is the size or culture, but it was very cold. It's very businesslike and I guess I'm not used to that...Coming from a small number of students, and coming to this school, was a big transition in more than one way. It was like from one extreme to another. If we are looking at intellectual abilities, size, everything was just bigger and different so there was a lot of adjustment.

Karen's first year was also challenging because of contrasts between her helping role as a guidance counselor and her disciplinary role as an administrator. Her interactions with students, staff, and parents were primarily negative because of her responsibility for safety and discipline. Karen spoke to some of the areas of adjustment on the job. Her interactions with students were mostly limited to those who were experiencing difficulty, and she missed the positive relationships she developed in the classroom.

> I like the challenges. I missed the classroom because I loved getting to know all of the students. But you get to know certain ones, but usually the ones that need the most help unfortunately. You don't get to know the good ones.

Dealing with parent and staff demands was also a source of difficulty because of gaps in her knowledge base related to the school culture and administrative protocols. In addition, her primarily middle-class parent body often bypassed her authority and appealed to the principal directly. Teaching staff often refused to take responsibility for their actions and downloaded their disciplinary problems by sending them to the office. She illustrated:

> We have had staff that send kids down because they didn't do their homework. Just the other day, a staff member complained to me that the kids are stealing her books from her cupboard. Like these workbooks that they have to pay for...So I say, "Tell me what's going on. How is this happening?" Eventually, it came out that she was leaving the room to photocopy stuff and the cupboard doors were always open. She never locks them. And I am going, "Well, let's try something preventive here." Like teachers expect us to solve their problems. You sort of have to look back and go, "OK why is this happening?"

She described long days which were consumed by paperwork and problem solving and evenings which were dedicated to reading e-mails at home. In time she came to accept that this was the nature of her school and job. She observed:

> The other part was just the number of staff that came to the door. . .Just getting used to that. Trying to stay on top of things, I found that difficult. And someone did say to me that as an administrator, you're never on top of things. So that took a while to sink in. Like I always felt bad because I didn't know what was going on, but in a school this size you never do.

As a third year assistant principal, Karen expressed satisfaction at her involvement in some of the leadership programs in her school. She believed that her job became less difficult because she had developed an understanding of the culture and structure of her school. She was also proud that she had been able to build more positive interactions with her staff in spite of their initial aloofness. She commented:

> It took a long time of, probably, schmoozing. Someone said to me at one time, "You know, when you go to a new school, the people you get to know first are your secretaries and the caretakers", and I worked on that first. Then the teaching staff eventually came along. I think being out in the hall all the time and trying to visit departments saying "Hi". I think I broke through that barrier.

In addition to focusing on student success initiatives, she was intentionally using her former experience in special education to assist teachers to design more inclusive curriculum:

> Yes, there are a lot of high achievers, but there are also those at the other end of the scale that need more support. And, how do we get that in place?

However, in spite of these collaborative relationships with staff, Karen experienced feelings of isolation throughout her transition because her role demands and her fears of "not getting caught up" inhibited her ability to get out of the school to interact with other administrators. She commented: "You need to connect. You sort of feel isolated here. I find I can't get out as much, so we have to try to connect somehow."

As she reflected on her transition, Karen reported that she enjoyed being an assistant principal in spite of her ongoing challenges:

> I like the challenges. I like dealing with the students, even the difficult ones. It's sort of a learning curve for me to keep up, like how do I deal with this situation? I love problem solving. I deal with puzzles at home all the time. How do I apply that?

While her job met some of her earlier expectations to support staff and students, ongoing changes due to district- and school-related reforms continued to be a challenge:

> I sort of knew what I was getting into, but on the other hand, with the political situation out there, it keeps changing. So I think you have to be flexible and keep adapting. Like, how can I deal with this situation?

She expressed some reservations about the possibility of effecting change due to the size of her school and ongoing issues in her school district, and she was planning on pursuing a principalship position in the near future.

Andrew's Story

> Education is all about people, and not only the students are people. I'm a human being too. What happened to preparing me before throwing me into a real life situation where I have to handle fights? I have to handle conflict resolution because of all these different things... even among teachers.

Andrew came to the assistant principalship from a leadership background in computers and business. He described his school as middle class and highly academic, with a strong staff of over 100 teachers and a motivated student body of 1,500. Andrew was in his third year as an assistant principal when our conversation started, and he was not sure exactly why he became an assistant principal. As he discussed his career pathway, Andrew identified a combination of personal and professional factors which influenced his decision making. These included his desire for a new challenge, the belief that he would be able to serve students, parents, and teachers on a larger scale, and the fact that other family members were also administrators. He was also inspired by the leadership of a former principal who pushed him to apply for promotion:

> Then I also was looking for more challenges, and one time I had a very inspiring principal who planted the seed in my head in the very early days when I was still teaching. So that gave me the initiative to explore what it was like on the other side of the desk.

Andrew approached the assistant principalship pathway with enthusiasm. He supplemented his university certification courses with school and district professional development opportunities and leadership activities. He also decided to "get his feet wet" by filling in as an acting assistant principal when one of his administrators became ill:

> So, I had a taste of it while I was doing the principals' course. It was a bit more hands-on, as opposed to the purely theoretical/conceptual work from the principals' program.

However, in spite of his preparation, Andrew encountered a number of surprises and roadblocks during his first year. His early days on the job were overwhelming and exhausting, and he was dogged by feelings of insecurity as he tried to negotiate unfamiliar locations, systems, tasks, and people. Looking back on his first week as an assistant principal, Andrew recalled with amusement:

> That was quite a nightmare. I think the neighborhood was so welcoming, that in fact it included all those students we kicked out of the school. So, all of a sudden, I have this big line up all the way back around the office. And they are all lined up to see me for admission. They want to plead their case. They want to ask for a second chance, so they all line up to see me. I was not really familiar with how the system worked. The first week when I came here, I was pretty much on my own, seeing these kids, taking down notes. "Alright, OK, I'll let you know." I didn't want to say no right away. I didn't know their background and I didn't want to be biased. So I spent all the time, day after day interviewing, meeting with all these students and their parents. And I felt that something was not quite right because when I looked to the other side of the office, I wondered, "How come the other vice-principal has no line?" Just me.

In the end, Andrew was able to resolve his problem by talking to his principal who advised him to ask the other assistant principal for assistance. He also contacted the assistant principal whom he replaced, and she provided him with the names of students with poor disciplinary and/or academic records whom he was required to interview before allowing them to come back:

> So, at the end I had no choice but to phone her to get some names. She left me with a list, but then some of them were not on the list. So she would know whether there was some validity there. So I jotted down a bunch of names and she was kind enough to drop by here on her way home. She was very supportive in that way, and I was thankful for her help. Looking back, it was very chaotic. I didn't have lunch until about five or six o'clock. I went home very tired, and didn't know what I had accomplished.

Andrew had also entered administration under the misconception that he could always return to his teaching position if he did not want to remain in administration. However, when he attempted to return he was shocked to learn that, although provincial legislation required administrators to pay to maintain a teaching certificate, they could not belong to teacher's unions or retain their teacher seniority. As he reflected on the professional and salary implications of his decision, Andrew became more frustrated:

> No one told me about it during the whole time when I was doing the Principals Course. No one discussed that. When I took on the appointment I said, "Well, if I don't like it I can always go back", and I was told by the principal, "No, you cannot." I said, "What? What do you mean I cannot? Of course I can. I am a member of the College of Teachers, am I not? Legally, I'm still a teacher. Who took that right from me?" So, why should someone be penalized because they would like to be more involved in leadership? I find that it is sad.

The lack of leadership opportunities was an ongoing tension for Andrew while negotiating and adjusting to his role as an assistant principal. During his three years as an assistant principal, he missed the energy of his classroom and the satisfaction of working collegially with students and staff. Describing the assistant principalship as a "dumping ground", he expressed concern regarding senior officials' lack of respect for assistant principals:

> I think the time, the workload, and the feeling that we are not really appreciated. Not so much really from the parents, but from the Board. The continuous downloading of work. . .. I am not really discounting the importance of the principal, but the brunt of the work goes all the way down to the vice-principal.

In spite of working long hours, Andrew found it difficult to fulfil his expectations of change and leadership because of external time pressures and the number of tasks which he was expected to accomplish. However, as he looked back on his transition, he believed he was managing well relative to other administrators he knew. Andrew emphasized the need to balance the positive and negative aspects of his role. He has been able to use his business, curriculum leadership, and parenting skills to improve his school, and he has built strong relationships with members of his administrative team.

Andrew identified significant passage milestones which reinforced his determination to find ways to support parents, staff, and students. The first occurred during the first year of his transition when a couple invited him to dinner at their home because of his assistance in working with their difficult son. He was also proud to be able to use his Asian heritage and his cultural knowledge to support and counsel students and parents from similar backgrounds who were underserved within the school system. Although these interventions contributed to long days and took time away from his family, he believed that it was an important part of his leadership role and he derived satisfaction from it:

> I was really surprised in the very beginning, when I met with some of these parents, that my language ability could make such a big difference in their just coming to the school and expressing themselves. Even grown men would actually cry in the office because they just felt so helpless.

Andrew's second milestone related to a conflict with a veteran staff member, which made him realize that, although he still identified with the teaching staff, they viewed him as an administrator. In spite of his attempts to work closely with faculty and his success with mentoring new teaching faculty, he encountered ongoing resistance from veterans who did not trust him because of his administrative status:

> Even though you try to approach it in a very delicate manner, there is that shield right there and everything they say to you is so guarded. And that's difficult to deal with, because that's not what I am here for. I am here also to make sure that we can resolve that issue.

Although he was in his third year as a vice-principal, Andrew still experienced the job as overwhelming and never-ending. In spite of working long hours, he found it difficult to fulfill his own and others' expectations because of the volume of tasks that he had to accomplish:

> There is the pressure of time. Quite often, I feel that I still haven't done enough. I feel that I am constantly behind. That's not a very good feeling. Getting back to the teachers, I have to say, yes, again, I can improve on that but it's the time. I want to get back to them right away. But sometimes, even leaving here around six or seven o'clock, I still can't get back to them. You know, writing them a memo or leaving them a note, there's just not enough time or support for that.

In spite of these challenges, Andrew believed he was managing well in the role relative to other assistant principals. Although he was unsuccessful in accomplishing all the things he set out to do initially, he was able to implement some changes. Here, he summarized some of his key learnings over the past 2 years:

> I learned this the last two years from the former principal here. You can basically kill someone with kindness. So always be courteous, be professional, and I have to keep reminding myself, especially when I am dealing with teachers, that I have to work together, day after day, year after year as a team. It is easier to win them over than trying to reshape them. Work with what you've got. I have learned to accept that.

Andrew expressed a commitment to support his community in spite of these roadblocks. In addition to working with a student leadership group, he used his technological and business expertise to integrate technology into his school's curriculum:

> Helping students and parents and being able to help teachers. That's my major satisfaction. For example, I am quite heavily involved with the IT of the school because of my background. And it really pleased me to see that I could help them so that they can have better equipment in their classrooms.

Having developed a more in-depth understanding of his school and his district's policies and procedures and having established a strong administrative network outside of school, Andrew was also exploring the possibility of becoming a principal and had already attended the district's promotion and placement information meetings.

Barb's Story

> I wish my heart had been harder. You know, don't take it personally. I wish I knew that I wasn't going to be able to have time to have lunch with my friends. I wish I knew that the most difficult part of the job was going to be the adult piece rather than the kid piece...I wish I knew it was OK to ask for help.

Barb was placed in an urban school of approximately 350 students and 40 teaching staff, where a majority of the students were identified as having learning and/or behavioral challenges. She described her parent and student populations as needy, because of stressors brought on by living with disabilities, deprived economic and social circumstances, and a general lack of knowledge about the workings of the school system. Our conversations began when she was in her third year as an assistant principal. Barb recalled making a conscious decision to pursue an administrative pathway when she switched from a business to a teaching career. This desire was motivated by a strong sense of social justice, a commitment to working with disenfranchised groups, and encouragement from a strong network of administrators within her district whom she could access for advice and resources.

Barb applied to the assistant principalship after completing the required teaching and certification requirements, and she was successful in her first round of interviews. Although she was excited by the prospect of being an administrator she experienced mixed feelings when she discovered that she had been assigned to a school where she had taught previously. While the school was a known entity, and she was delighted to be working with some of her close friends, she also knew that some of the staff members held grudges against her and doubted her competence. Her first year was emotionally and physically difficult because of challenges from staff and students and the pressure to prove her competence. She also described profound feelings of isolation and insecurity because she was unsure of whom she could trust:

> The loneliness [was a challenge], especially coming back to a school that I had taught at. So, it's, how do you fit in? You have a history with some of these people. They know who you are, they know how you work. Now, there is a little bit of pressure to perform as a vice-principal rather than a teacher.

Barb recalled feeling more comfortable by the end of the first year, and she was able to identify some progress when she compared her earlier and current approach to the demands of the job. She highlighted prioritizing the demands on her time as an important learning:

First, I would deal with things as they came. And, then you realize that some things are not as urgent as other things. I guess by failing, you realize what is more important. By watching other people, you realize it. By some sort of innate idea, you figure it out. So it goes from: What's urgent?; What needs to be taken care of right now?; and What it is that you can put off? I guess at the beginning, when the phone would ring, I would take that call immediately. So and so is calling, I need to take that call. The phone rings, I need to pick it up. Now, I'm a little more relaxed on that issue and I will do phone calls later. I will do emails later unless they are urgent. If it is a teacher who needs me in their room, that's an immediate thing. That I know. Somebody pages down, I need to go up there. If it's dealing with a kid, sometimes they need time to wait, so they have a little time to rest on the bench rather than talking to me immediately as they come in.

Barb experienced an unexpected sense of loss during her second year when two of her administrative colleagues left and they were replaced by a new principal and assistant principal. In addition, although she was more familiar with the building than they were, she often felt marginalized when her new principal made key decisions in conjunction with the other assistant principal without asking for Barb's input. She expressed nostalgia as she compared her previous relationship with the administrative team:

Year two, I was the old girl on campus, so that was different. I guess I was the person with the most knowledge of the building, but the two new people would collectively work together. So even though I was the person with the most knowledge, I found that I was out of the loop more with respect to the admin team. Whereas the first year, I think we worked more as a three person team together in decision making. We would make decisions at meetings. We wouldn't make decisions having a sidebar conversation over coffee. So that's different, the way the admin team was functioning in the second year.

During her second year, Barb also experienced a shift which she connected to her increased familiarity with the school culture and her assistant principal duties and routines. She believed that she was at a stage where she had mastered the tasks of the assistant principalship, and she attributed her changed perspective to the fact that she had established a positive reputation for herself and a foundation of clear expectations for staff and students:

I've built up enough trust. People know my work ethic. They know that they can count on me. There isn't any second-guessing by people anymore, of "Can she do the job?"

Barb expressed a great deal of pride in her ability to work with her school community to engage her students in leadership initiatives, in spite of their learning challenges. In addition to supporting a successful nutrition program and clothing drive, she has also worked with staff to implement curriculum initiatives related to literacy, numeracy, and life skills. She also mentored new teachers in their transition, and actively supported experienced faculty who were interested in applying for school and district leadership positions. By the time she had reached her third year, Barb had gradually extended her focus to include larger systemic issues and was involved in district-wide committees which focused on creating equitable learning opportunities and outcomes for students with special needs. Having been encouraged by her superintendent to apply for the principalship, she had already successfully completed her district's promotion rounds for this position and had been informed that she would be promoted the following year.

Chapter 4
Charting the Administrative Passage

Abstract Chapter 4 charts the administrative passage through the eyes of recently appointed assistant principals. It describes the external landscape – the different actors and contexts which newcomers encounter as well as the internal landscape – the cognitive, emotional, and behavioral processes that they experience as a result of these interactions. The assistant principals' narratives suggest that new administrators engage in a series of cyclical processes as they cross the boundary between teaching and administration. This chapter extends the transitional framework that was described in Chapter 1, and it provides a more extensive analysis of the complex dynamic which occurs when professional and organizational forces impact individual transitions. A metaphor of epicycles or cycles within cycles is introduced to illustrate the assistant principals' internal and external trajectory. The four cycles of Entry–Exit, Immersion–Emersion, Disintegration–Reintegration, and Transformation–Restabilization illustrate the paradoxical nature of the administrative change and transition passages and are presented from the assistant principals' insider perspective.

The profiles in the preceding chapter provided snapshots of the eight assistant principals' early organizational experiences and highlighted their reasons for becoming assistant principals, how they prepared for the role, the kinds of supports they received, the challenges they encountered, their general perceptions of the transition, and their future goals. While they arrived at the decision to become an administrator in different ways and at different life stages, these men and women all articulated a common goal of making a difference for students. They also assumed that the assistant principalship would allow them to make a more significant impact on the school system and that their passage would be predictable. As a result, they were surprised to find themselves at a critical career juncture between teaching and administration where a variety of unanticipated personal, professional, and organizational variables converged, presenting them with unexpected adaptation and adjustment challenges.

D.E. Armstrong, *Administrative Passages*, Studies in Educational Leadership 4,
DOI 10.1007/978-1-4020-5269-9_4, © Springer Science+Business Media B.V. 2009

Crossroads, Intersections, and Boundaries

When viewed as a composite, the assistant principals' individual stories reveal patterns which are consistent with previous research on new administrators' transitions within the fields of business (Dotlich et al., 2004; Hill, 1992) and education (Hartzell et al., 1994; Marshall & Hooley, 2006; Schmidt, 2000; Sigford, 1998). These studies show that although the promotion to administration is generally seen as a discrete, objective event from the organizational perspective, new administrators experience it as a destabilizing and subjective process. The unpredictability and stress of this upward move is captured by O'Connor and Wolfe (1991, p. 326), who state that, "Moving to a higher level of organization requires an extensive passage through uncertainty, much like re-designing the proverbial plane in flight." Freedman's (1998) description of the promotion to a frontline supervisory position also captures the stochastic nature of this role shift:

> The first-line supervisory role is not a straight–line extrapolation of the individual contributor's job. Rather, the promotion constitutes something like a 135-degree turn…newly promoted persons shift upward and move off – often unexpectedly, unplanned, and unprepared – in unprecedented directions into unfamiliar territory. (p. 137)

The assistant principals' narratives confirmed that the promotion from teacher to administrator opens up a complex internal and external landscape which is characterized by unexpected crossroads and boundaries and requires them to make critical pathway choices (Armstrong, 2005). Freedman's concept of crossroads and description of organizational socialization boundaries (Greenfield, 1985c; Louis, 1980; Schein, 1978) provide insight into the nature of the challenges that assistant principals encounter. According to Freedman (1998), crossroads consist of "discontinuous and unprecedented changes in the role responsibilities and accountabilities to which managers in transition must respond" (p. 137). Each level is unique and is characterized by the distinctive demands each one makes on the people who participate at that level. Assistant principals' crossroads are triggered when teachers deviate from their familiar landscape in order to pursue an administrative route. These crossroads are further intensified when administrative candidates are promoted to managerial positions and are required to navigate a cultural landscape which is radically different in size, scope, and complexity from their previous classroom environments.

Analyses of new administrators' experiences (Greenfield, 1985c; Louis, 1980; Schein, 1978) identify the existence of hidden boundaries within organizational socialization practices which are also consistent with Freedman's description of managerial crossroad challenges. Greenfield's (1985c) study of newly appointed school administrators highlights socialization boundaries which are ingrained within the hierarchical, functional, and inclusionary domains of organizations and which represent different dimensions of challenge and change. New and aspiring assistant principals encounter hierarchical boundaries as they cross from teaching or department headship positions to middle-management roles which entail supervising others and being supervised. They also have to learn to navigate functional boundaries as they master operational tasks such as supervising and monitoring students, personnel, instruction, facilities, and resources. In addition, they have to cross inclusionary boundaries in order to become an organizational insider and position themselves within their school's and district's information and influence network.

Organizational crossroads, intersections, and boundaries play an important function in defining the culture, climate, and topography of administration. Although they often represent taken-for-granted educational structures, they mask embedded paradoxes and dilemmas within administrative roles and relationships which are unrecognizable from the perspective of external stakeholders (Hartzell, et al., 1994; Marshall, 1992a, 1992b; Marshall & Hooley, 2006). They are also characterized by hidden rites, rituals, and ceremonies which mark the move from outsider to insider and between teaching and administrative roles. These processes reinforce and protect organizational roles and structures, and they communicate information about acceptable and unacceptable administrative behaviors and role boundaries. They test aspiring and new administrators physically, socially, and psychologically, and their individual and their aggregate effects shape educators' career pathways and administrative outcomes (Armstrong, in press-b).

New administrators experience separation rites, such as subtle shunning and polite silences from former teacher colleagues when the promotion is made public (Conway, 1990). Common separation rites and rituals also include parties, ceremonies, and assemblies which allow novices to exit their teacher role. Initiation rites also occur at the first staff meeting or school assembly when they are introduced to staff. Transition and incorporation rites include introductions to faculty at the first staff meeting, and humor tests that humiliate new administrators. New assistant principals also face trials, such as, organizing their first school assembly, creating the master schedule, doing their first suspension or expulsion, and dealing with challenges and criticism from different community stakeholders (Armstrong, in press-b). Novice assistant principals tend to be caught unawares by these rites, rituals, and ceremonies because pre-role preparation courses and school district induction seldom alert them to the technical, social, and emotionally charged nature of the middle-management landscape (Armstrong, 2002; Sigford, 1998).

The Administrative Landscape

The assistant principals' narratives suggest that administrative passages are made up of complex social and psychological dimensions that shape personal and professional roles and practices. Social dimensions pertain to the external landscape of groups, networks, memberships, and participation arenas, while psychological dimensions comprise the internal landscape of attitudes, feelings, perceptions, and the personal meanings and stories that are motivated by social relationships.

The External Dimensions

Although assistant principals' passages are often experienced as discrete, individual events, they are influenced by social, economic, and historical factors that are connected to the climate, topography, and culture of their local school and district. Cole and Knowles (2000) identify at least three levels of context that influence educators' work. These include the demographics and dynamics of the local community; the ways in which the various cultural and ethnic groups, parents, and corporate and business entities define educators' work and student learning; and the complex micro-political and psychosocial interactions between educational professionals, students, and community. These entities are also influenced by rapid organizational reforms, changing external societal standards, and technological advances which add to the complexity of the administrative passage.

Stakeholder Impacts

The assistant principals' frontline role also exposes them to a complicated network of individual and collective bodies both inside and outside of the school that impact their daily work. Teachers who aspire to be administrators are generally unaware of the vast range of constituents that they will be required to serve when they leave the confines of their classroom. While many anticipate working with students and adults within schools, they are often surprised by the number of additional stakeholder groups, such as the school and district's business office, district operations, and other district and school support staff who can who can make or break their day. Even more surprising are the overwhelming number of individuals and groups outside of the school, such as, social workers, police officers, local politicians, and other members of the surrounding community who impact their role and their ability to support students.

Figure 4.1 provides a picture of key stakeholders who comprise the assistant principals' external context. Each of these stakeholder groups lays its own peculiar claim to the social and political organizational terrain and exerts its socializing pressure on new assistant principals to protect their interests. Hidden environmental factors such as the climate of the school, staff attitudes, and community expectations also pervade the school context. These external factors constitute multiple layers of influence, which impose competing socializing pressures on novice administrators. When combined, they exert a powerful influence which helps to determine how new assistant principals interpret and enact their leadership role.

Within the physical boundaries of their assigned school, new assistant principals interact with students, along with a variety of employee groups ranging from teaching and support staff to members of their administrative team. While the socializing impact of students is often neglected in the literature because they are not seen to be as powerful as the adults within the school hierarchy, students, by their sheer numbers alone, have the power to control assistant principals' workdays because of the latter's disciplinary responsibilities. Matthews and Crow (2003) indicate that, "New administrators sometimes surprisingly forget that students have an incredible influence on the culture and climate of the school and can thus strongly influence the learning of new school leaders" (p. 265). Students' conceptions of the management and discipline aspects of the assistant principals' functions can also influence how novices enact their role. Like the adults in the building, students communicate

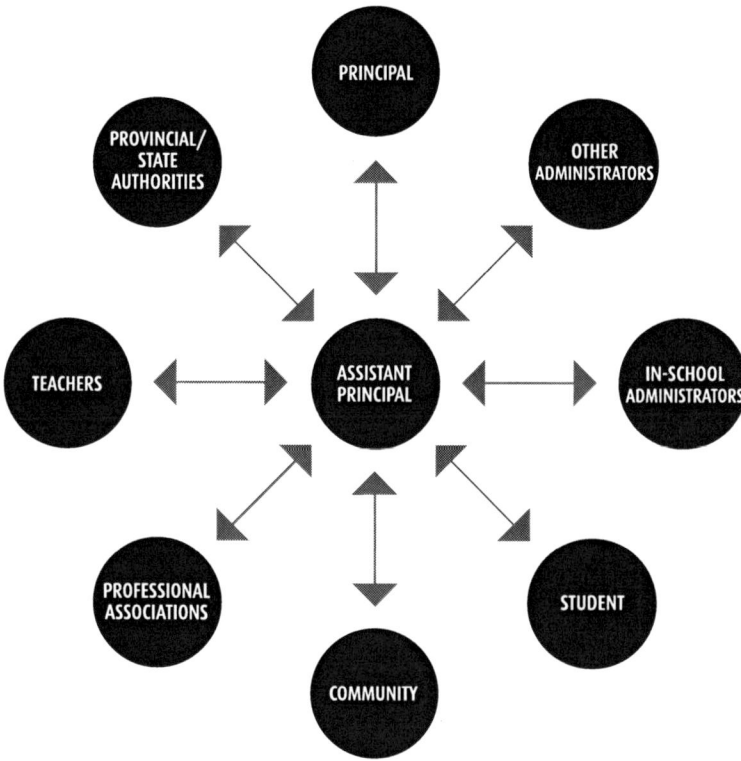

Fig. 4.1 The external landscape

certain expectations about assistant principals' roles, reinforcing normative images of authority and rejecting inconsistencies.

School principals are often identified as a key source of influence because of their power to assign assistant principals' duties and to evaluate them. Principals also influence transitions by providing or denying support, encouragement, advice, and mentoring, as well as sponsorship for future careers (Malone, 2001; Matthews & Crow, 2003; Playko & Daresh, 1993). Veteran assistant principals can also wield a tremendous amount of power over newcomers because they possess the institutional knowledge related to the structure, culture, and technology of the school, the student body, and the various employee groups. However, in some schools, this information is sometimes withheld from newcomers as part of the administrative rites of passage (Armstrong, in press-a). In addition, new assistant principals are generally delegated the most difficult and less interesting tasks by the principal and other senior administrative team members (Marshall, 1992a, Playko & Daresh, 1993). Administrative team dynamics can have a debilitating effect on newcomers who do not conform to the ethos of the team. In schools where there are more than two assistant principals the aggregate effect of the administrative team can create a competitive ethic (Armstrong, 2002).

Although some theorists (e.g., Playko & Daresh, 1993) identify principals as the key source of assistant principal socialization, Matthews and Crow (2003) suggest that teachers also can be a powerful source of influence. As a collective, they also wield a tremendous amount of power because of their unions. Veteran staff, in particular, often possess and control the type of information assistant principals need in order to make decisions, and they are likely to protect this information until they believe they can trust novices. Although new assistant principals are generally drawn from the teaching ranks, they are often overwhelmed by teachers' political power and their different departmental and group agendas. Competing teacher factions within the school may also communicate different and conflicting demands. Matthews and Crow (2003) caution that, "A typical early mistake of new administrators is to view teachers as a unitary group, when in fact there are frequently various subcultures and groups of teachers who hold conflicting expectations for the principal" (p. 265). While most new assistant principals develop confidence over time in resolving conflicts with students, parents, and other community members regarding their role, they experience ongoing frustration when confronted with the range and number of different teachers' expectations for the role of assistant principal.

Working with their school's business and operations staff in a supervisory capacity is also an uncharted area for new assistant principals. Although business and operations staff, such as secretaries and caretakers are fewer in number, and do not carry the same institutional and professional clout as teachers, they can also exert a strong socializing influence on assistant principals. Office secretaries are often the first agents of socialization because of their proximity to assistant principals and their role in orienting novices to their duties. Veteran office staff possess a wealth of tacit knowledge and historical information about the school and the yearly cycle which are important for the effective running of school, but are hidden from teaching faculty and inexperienced administrators. In many cases, assistant principals develop a closer level of attachment and trust with their secretaries than they do with teachers.

Parents and other community members are influential external sources of socialization, particularly because of their increased power due to recent reform measures and legislative changes related to school governance and accountability. Administrators outside the assistant principal's school are additional sources of socialization because they can provide valuable support and encouragement, reinforce the status quo, or encourage and support new images of the role (Calebrese & Tucker-Ladd, 1991; Hartzell et al., 1994). District supervisors, such as school superintendents and trustees, are also significant influences because they control resources and can limit or foster assistant principals' autonomy by overriding or supporting decisions they have made. In addition, these individuals have the power to select, promote, hire, evaluate, sanction, and dismiss (Calebrese, 1991; Hartzell, 1991, 1993; Marshall, 1985a; Scoggins & Bishop, 1993). When combined, these external groups provide a potent and often conflicted socializing force that shapes the external contours of new administrators' passages and their eventual leadership pathways.

The Internal Dimensions

Researchers who examine individual change, transitions, and passages identify a complex internal network of thoughts, emotions, feelings, values, beliefs, and assumptions which are also influenced by the passage itself, as well as by changes in the external context. Sheehy (2006) connects both internal and external domains and she observes that, "The inner realm is where the crucial shifts in bedrock begin to throw a person off balance, signaling the necessity to change and move to a new footing in the next stage of development" (p. 30). Studies of new administrators' experiences also establish a correspondence between hierarchical organizational role changes and shifts in their internal landscape. Louis (1980) proposes that the promotion to a managerial role creates dissonance because of disjunctions between newcomers' anticipations and the reality of the administrative landscape. This destabilizes the individual's psychological field and motivates corresponding adjustments at the cognitive level. O'Connor and Wolfe (1991) equate this process with a paradigm shift which entails questioning fundamental assumptions. They point out that:

> As the grip of the old paradigm loosens, the rules, methods and norms governing one's life, so ingrained and taken for granted, become foci of attention and concern. A questioning of beliefs, values, feelings and knowledge may take place. As past formulas fail or succeed less well, a search for new arrangements results. (p. 326)

Schmidt et al. (1998a, 1998b) show that new administrators experience perspective, behavior, and personality changes that impact their practice and outlook. Greenfield (1985a) also identifies cognitive and behavioral changes during administrative candidacy that emerge from organizational socialization processes and are consistent with the development of an "administrative perspective," i.e., a psychological shift in affect, values, dispositions, thought patterns, and actions.

Although the majority of studies tend to focus on the cognitive and behavioral shifts, there is strong evidence that these changes trigger a complex range of emotional responses. Schmidt (2000) observes, "When educators' responsibilities shift, so do their emotions – particularly those emotions for which they may not have been prepared or forewarned" (p. 840). In addition to identifying changes in assumptions and beliefs, Viney (1980) confirms that a transition "is rarely purely cognitive but has to do with feelings and beliefs as well as thoughts" (p. 17). Emotions are important transitional mediators; they facilitate the development of new assumptions and beliefs that allow individuals to create intelligible patterns and integrate changes into their lives (Bridges, 2001). These shifts generally lead to a questioning of personal and professional worldviews and practice, and provoke changes at the cognitive, emotional, and spiritual levels which result in new perspectives and changed identities (Bridges, 2001, 2003; Daloz, 2000).

Aporias, Dilemmas, and Crises of Meaning

Although the promotion to administration is generally regarded as a celebratory event, it provokes both negative and positive feelings (Armstrong, 2004b; Dotlich et al., 2004; Hartzell et al., 1994; Marshall, 1992a,1992b; Sigford, 1998). A number of studies identify responses that accompany major changes, including emotions such as shock, sadness, fear, and anger, thoughts such as dismay and disbelief, and behaviors such as panic and immobility (Hill, 1992; Marshall, 1992a; Sigford, 1998). These unfamiliar thoughts and emotions often compete with or contradict new administrators' deeply held values and beliefs, and may lead to feelings of disequilibrium as well as physical and social dislocation (Armstrong, 2004b; Louis, 1980; Sigford, 1998).

As new administrators attempt to restore balance to their personal and professional worlds, they experience crises of meaning that are consistent with Burbules' (1997) conception of pathway aporias (Armstrong, 2004b). Drawing on Sarah Kaufman's distinction between the two Greek words for "pathway," *odos* and *poros*, Burbules (1997) provides a useful illustration of the different types of pathways that can be applied to assistant principals' transitional trajectories. He describes an *odos* as a familiar road that connects two knowns and proceeds in a fixed direction. Such passages are predictable; they often come with maps or directions, and they hold few surprises or challenges. The second type of pathway, a *poros*, is a road that leads to an unknown destination. This type of route involves a passage across a chaotic expanse or uncharted territory, and it requires creating a trail where one does not exist.

The absence of a clear path toward an unknown destination provokes an aporia as a crisis of choice, belief, action, or identity.[1] Aporias are characterized by doubt, discomfort, uncertainty, and confusion and they impact individuals on multiple levels simultaneously. Individuals in a state of aporia may lack both the knowledge and the understanding of their landscape, i.e., a conceptual map or step-by-step algorithm of how they got there, or a sense of their relative location within a "network of possibilities" (p. 2). Burbules explains:

> Aporia is an experience that affects us on many levels at once: we feel discomfort, we doubt ourselves. We may ask "What do I do?" "What do I say?" "Who am I?" "What is my relation to others?" (p. 2)

Burbules' depiction of aporia coheres with previous descriptions of transitional and transformational crises (Abrego & Brammer, 1992; Bridges, 1980; Mezirow, 2000; Van Gennep, 1960). A common element in these analyses is the emergence of a disorienting dilemma that is triggered by internal and/or external change events.

---

[1] Burbules (1997) focuses on the transitional state of *aporia* that is derived from Plato's dialogue, the *Meno*, where Socrates is teaching a young boy a geometry lesson. When the boy's initial guess is wrong, Socrates leads him through a step-by-step line of argument (*elenchus*) to the realization that his guess must be incorrect. The moment of aporia occurs when a misconception has been exposed and where a clean terrain now exists for the reconstruction of true knowledge.

Disorienting dilemmas evoke cognitive, emotional, spiritual, and existential discomfort and may also include feelings of excitement, denial, fear, anger, or shame. They are often accompanied by a period of self-examination that motivates individuals to examine, validate, and revise previous perspectives and habits of mind, and to explore and experiment with new roles and options (Cranton, 2006; Kegan, 2000; King, 2005; Mezirow, 2000). Assistant principals experience existential and epistemic aporias when they cross personal, professional, and organizational boundaries and are unable to reconcile the reality of the administrative landscape with their teaching worlds and expectations. Their attempts to resolve these challenges precipitate an intensive journey across the external organizational landscape, as well as the internal domain of the self.

This journey is consistent with previous findings about transition and transformational processes. Taylor's (2000) analysis of research studies that focus on transformation found that individual transformation tends to be a recursive, evolving, fluid, and spiraling process. He noted that "the journey of transformation is less linear in nature than recursive, such that several phases are repeated as one is transformed" (p. 291). Bridges (1980, 2001) also indicates that transition and transformational cycles do not always occur in fixed and progressive steps or in a smooth, continuous pattern and that individuals may be in one or more transition cycles. Each cycle has its own distinctive qualities and inner stability and requires mastery of certain developmental tasks. Cycles may also blend into one another, overlap, and repeat in a continuous process (Abrego & Brammer, 1992; Brammer, 1991; Nicholson & West, 1988).

Epicycles and Transformational Trajectories

A metaphor of transitional epicycles,[2] a constellation of cycles within cycles (Armstrong, 2004a), provides a visual representation of the assistant principals' trajectory from teaching to administration. Each epicycle describes the internal and external topography of the administrative landscape by contextualizing the psychological process of change and transition within the social environment. Figure 4.2 depicts the iterative nature of this change process and the assistant principals' internal change and transformation trajectory as it evolves within the external organizational landscape. This transformational model is person-centered in order to represent the

---

[2]Originally Ptolemy used epicycles to explain the motions of the planets in a geocentric solar system. He assumed that the earth was at the center of the solar system, and proposed a theory to explain the complex motion of the planets and the sun based on this flawed assumption. While the underlying assumption is flawed, and therefore Ptolemy's theory is also false, his model can be extended to other contexts. Just as Ptolemy's model attempted to explain a geocentric view of the solar system, the model above provides an egocentric view of a transformational environment. The analogy between Ptolemy's model and the proposed transformational model is further strengthened by the increasing complex trajectories that can be described by relatively simple compound motion in the egocentric view.

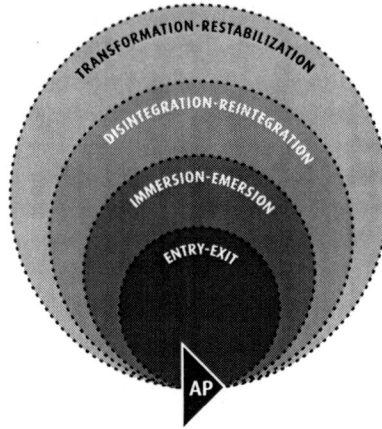

Fig. 4.2 Epicycles of transition and transformation

new administrators' location within the change cycle, and it describes the increasingly complex administrative trajectory as perceived from the individual's basic egocentric viewpoint.

In Fig. 4.2 the assistant principals' trajectory from teaching to administration is portrayed as a series of four concentric cycles. These epicycles chart the iterative trajectory of the assistant principal undergoing transformational change within a non-static environment such as a school. The successive phases of the transition are conceptualized as a constellation of epicycles, which is generated as each phase of the new assistant principal's trajectory builds on the previous cycles. The newly appointed assistant principal is positioned in the middle of the transitional cycle to indicate the onset of the transition and his or her centrality to the change process.

At first glance, the visual representation of the four concentric circles conveys an image of simplicity, cyclical uniformity, and forward progression. In a sense, this illusion of stability mirrors outsiders' assumptions that the pathway from teaching to administration is smooth and straightforward. However, in spite of its external appearance of stability, the assistant principals confirmed that while this professional trajectory was initially perceived as linear from their teaching standpoint, upon entering the administrative passage, it was experienced as a chaotic process from their egocentric vantage point.

The four epicycles trace the inner and outer dimensions of the administrative transition, i.e., the cognitive, emotional, and social processes that assistant principals go through as they move from being a teacher to becoming and being an administrator. This simultaneous analysis of individual characteristics and external circumstances highlights the dialectical relationship between the assistant principal and the passage. This is a mutually reinforcing dynamic that is shaped by, and shapes, the interactions between assistant principals and their schools. The names of the four epicycles – *Exit–Entry, Immersion–Emersion, Disintegration–*

Reintegration, Transformation–Restabilization – communicate the paradoxical nature of this transformative process and the potential for both retrograde and forward progression. The iterative nature of these interconnected loops generates a cyclical dynamic which feeds experiences back on themselves to create new cycles. The dotted lines represent the semipermeable nature of epicycles and the ability to move back and forth between cycles.

The first or primary circle, *Entry–Exit*, represents the local or first-order trajectory when the aspiring assistant principals were still teachers, and their perception of the administrative pathway was one of relative constancy and simplicity. The second-order trajectory, *Immersion–Emersion*, is represented by a secondary circle that evolves from the point that is generated when the newly appointed assistant principals undertake their new role. Although both motions are simple progressions, when overlaid, they were perceived as complex from the assistant principals' first-order egocentric view because of the shocks and surprises that occurred as a result of their encounter with the administrative landscape. This is increasingly true for higher-order trajectories when viewed from the first-order egocentric vantage point. However, as the new assistant principals move to higher orders of egocentric perception, such as the *Disintegration–Reintegration*, or *Transformation–Restabilization* cycles, they are able to look back on the simple motions that comprised the lower-order egocentric perceptions of the trajectory and, in doing so, develop a clearer perspective of the change and transition passage being undertaken.

It is important to note that although there are some broad general patterns to the transformational epicycles, they are also an idiosyncratic process. Each assistant principal goes through the cycles in varying ways and within different time frames depending on pre- and post-transition ecological factors related to personality characteristics, individual dispositions, role preparation, support, and school contexts. Epicycles represent a cumulative process and each phase of the trajectory builds on the individual's previous cycles. Movement to the next phase is contingent on the assistant principal's ability to resolve issues in the previous cycle. The individual's administrative passage is constructed and reconstructed through a negotiated personal and organizational process which is scaffolded by his or her internal thoughts and feelings and interactions with their external environment. In essence, the assistant principal is the channel for the passage, is journeying on the passage, and is also an inseparable part of the terrain. Although he or she can look back on the territory covered, he/she cannot step outside of the boundaries of the experience. The dynamic which emerges from the tensile state of being and becoming carries possibilities for growth and development. As the assistant principals' narratives attest, even the most stable condition of *Transformation–Restabilization* embodies the possibility of future change and a new transitional cycle. Chapters 5, 6, 7, and 8 provide in-depth descriptions of each phase of the assistant principals' trajectory.

Chapter 5
Entry–Exit: Crossing the Administrative Threshold

Abstract This chapter focuses on the cycle of Entry–Exit, which marks the beginning of the administrative passage. It discusses the new assistant principals' reasons for becoming assistant principals, their pre-role preparation, and the strategies they use in order to create an administrative pathway. The threshold tensions, dilemmas, and rites of passage that the novices experience as they leave their teaching role and enter administrative territory are also described.

The first cycle of the assistant principals' trajectory, Entry–Exit, is triggered during their teaching career when they decide to pursue the administrative pathway, and it ends shortly after they leave teaching and assume their new administrative role. Aspiring assistant principals arrive at the administrative threshold through a wide variety of routes, and their decision to pursue this pathway is often related to a combination of both personal and professional reasons. They may receive encouragement and support from family and friends, as well as teaching colleagues and administrative sponsors. Most administrative candidates are also motivated by a strong desire to undertake a new professional challenge. They believe that they will make a difference to staff and students, as well as their own career, and they often assume that they will make a direct and simple transfer from teaching to administration.

However, the assistant principals' narratives show that becoming an administrator is neither a straightforward crossover nor a linear, predictable process. Rather, the road to administration is a spiraling pathway, which is made up of surprising twists and turns. Entry–Exit is an important critical personal and organizational checkpoint where aspiring administrators encounter early passage rites and decision-making crossroads. Aspiring administrators are often unaware that administrative entry also entails a complementary psychological and social process of exit from teaching which triggers hidden social and psychological processes. Unexpected detours, mixed signals, and roadblocks are the norm, and newcomers experience mixed emotions as they navigate the social and emotional crossroads between teaching and administration.

Forging a Pathway

As they reflected on this pre-administrative arrival period, the eight assistant principals identified finding a direct route to administration as one of their major challenges. Although crossing over appeared simple on the surface, they were surprised to find that they had to carve their own route, and in some cases, they were unsure about how and where to get information about how to do this.

Without clear maps or mentors to provide them with step-by-step guidance toward an administrative route, the assistant principals often felt at a loss navigating the administrative threshold. This frustration which accompanied this aporia of direction is captured in Michael's comment:

> What is it that I need to do? Who do I need to talk to, to help me get to where I want to get? And I just happened to ask enough people questions. I haven't really had anyone say, "Oh, Michael, you want to be a vice-principal, take, this and this and this." My last principal, if there was anything that came by his desk, he would feed it to me. But there was nobody clearly defining the path for me.

Determining how to disengage from teaching and move ahead within the organizational hierarchy motivated the aspiring assistant principals to survey the organizational landscape and to engage in a variety activities which would allow them to chart their promotion route.

Threshold Rites

Developing maps of the administrative territory required that the assistant principals consciously and unconsciously engage in threshold orienteering rites and rituals which allowed them to exit teaching while building the groundwork for their promotion pathway. One of the assistant principals' key threshold tasks was the building of cognitive and social maps. Cognitive maps help individuals to learn the norms of their work environment, as well as the rules and reinforcers that regulate their roles (Nicholson & West, 1988). These are complemented by social maps, which allow administrative candidates to determine the social and political networks that can facilitate their successful entry into administration.

The assistant principals' descriptions of the process of developing cognitive and social maps were consistent with earlier studies of professional and organizational socialization (Armstrong, 2002; Ashforth, 2001; Greenfield, 1985a). These activities included weighing the positive and negative aspects of teaching and administrative roles, observing administrators, asking questions in order to develop a more in-depth understanding of administration, and making connections with individuals who could help them navigate the administrative threshold. These threshold rites allow aspiring administrators to gain membership and acceptance within the administrative reference group and to cross inclusionary boundaries. They are an important part of anticipatory socialization processes, and they facilitate the development of a positive orientation toward administration, and the internalization of its values and dispositions (Greenfield, 1985a).

The assistant principals' threshold rites and rituals included formal and informal socialization tasks. Formal tasks were primarily related to completing mandated professional certification and school district selection and hiring processes. As part of their trajectory toward administration, the assistant principals completed their professional certification during their teaching tenure and they took an average of 3–4 years of academic preparation to complete the requirements. These certification courses functioned as a formal and collective means of professional socialization where the administrative candidates met off-site as part of a heterogeneous group of teachers from different school districts.

Overall, these formal processes were fairly predictable. The candidates were required to meet a straightforward set of outcomes, and they felt empowered to exert some control over the process. For the most part, the course curriculum was presented from an organizational perspective through traditional theories of principal leadership and was taught by principals. For assistant principals like Michael, who were not fully committed to the administrative pathway, this formal socialization period was a critical choice point. However, his enthusiasm was increased when he was encouraged to apply for promotion by fellow course participants:

> And as I got into that, I got more information or learned more and it started to be more appealing. I met a whole bunch of other leaders. And we talked about why they got into it and why I was kind of going through the motions, and they kind of gave me a little bit of a push, because their passion kind of caught on.

However, while the prerequisite principals' certification courses provided valuable information about the principalship and leadership theories, they failed to prepare these administrative candidates for the technical and sociopolitical challenges of the job. Andrew identified the lack of preparation as a key contributor to the emotional strain that the new assistant principals experienced:

> A lot of the skills that are required as an administrator haven't been touched when we go through the Principals' programs. I remember the first several weeks that feeling of inadequacy really puts you down.

Some of the respondents also pointed out that although the certification requirements were articulated in provincial and district policies, they included hidden informal subprocesses. For example, teachers who were "tapped on the shoulder" were more likely to receive information about the timelines and prerequisite courses directly from their supervisors, who also provided advice regarding how to map their approach and the kinds of shortcuts they could take. Additional by-products of formal certification processes were the informal opportunities they provided for participants to create alliances with experienced administrative mentors and other administrative candidates who were also forging their own pathway to administration. These relationships built the foundation for future networks inside and outside of their school and district, and a number of the assistant principals used their connections to support their future administrative journey.

The aspiring administrators also discovered that they had to fulfil a number of informal rites at the school and district levels in order to be selected to move on to the next level of the pathway. Unlike the formal certification rites, these requirements were not explicitly articulated, and they did not have fixed timelines or outcomes. They also varied by individual and school culture. An important part of these socialization rituals entailed a process of Getting the Attention of Superiors or GASing (Griffiths, Goldman, & MacFarland, as cited in Greenfield, 1977). Building a credible leadership profile and positioning themselves to be noticed by supervisors entailed assuming additional responsibilities at the school and district levels, which demonstrated their interest in and suitability for administration and get their principal's and superintendent's sponsorship. As a result, in addition to their teaching and departmental responsibilities, the aspiring assistant principals communicated their interest by volunteering for additional administrative duties.

The assistant principals' stories revealed differential practices within their schools which impacted their transitional experiences. Teachers who were groomed as potential leaders were sponsored to attend professional development courses and were asked to assume positions of responsibility related to chairing committees, substituting for absent administrators, student and staff scheduling, attendance counseling, and committee leadership. Commenting on his entry experiences, Greg observed:

> I was very fortunate. I was in on teacher interviews – for the last three or four years I was invited in as one of the team leaders to do that. And being in a very inclusive administrative team with the previous three principals, I always felt part of it. And with our former board having the earlier model of team leaders where we made decisions in terms of budget, staff allocation, and timetabling. So there was an easing in to this process, which was great.

Similarly, as the Head of Guidance, Karen's physical proximity to the main office and her close working relationship with the administrative team allowed her to demonstrate her knowledge of administrative tasks such as scheduling, grade reporting, student registration, garnering her supervisor's support.

Administrative candidates who were well positioned regarded these opportunities as important in allowing them to build administrative experience and to network with supervisory colleagues. Conversely, aspirants like Sandy, Esther, and Jerry who were not on the inside track perceived these practices as random and inequitable and they felt disadvantaged by these informal processes. While Sandy believed that assuming more active roles as a curriculum leader and participating in a variety of committees earned the respect of her school community and the administrative team, she expressed disappointment at the lack of support she received relative to other White, male candidates. Here, she describes a process of being "recognized, but not fully supported":

> Certainly all the leadership stuff I did. And I did great leadership things in the school, I got profile and benefits and so on, and I was recognized for that. I mean, how could you not? You can't! But, I didn't get that kind of concrete help. And I would see others, two others, who went through the process at the same time, but were treated differently. For example, one particular person who had gone through the process with me would be called up to be given office experience, when somebody was out of the office, although we were both in the

same position. I remember once I walked into a conversation when this person was being called up, and I wasn't supposed to overhear that, and it was kind of hush–hush. And I think one time I was called, and I think it was partly because I had overheard that conversation. So you know it is subtle things like that. Or when we are going through the process, that big practicum piece, you are supposed to demonstrate great leadership and bust your butt. And I would compare myself to one particular person, and I'm not exaggerating, who absolutely did nothing!

Although this differential treatment increased her frustration and lack of trust of her administrative supervisors, realizing that she was on the outside of the circle of influence motivated her to work harder:

And I'm thinking, like, you get kind of frustrated because I have always approached things thinking that, "I can't make any assumptions that I'm going to get an easy ride." So when I go inside, I go in full, and I'm doing everything I'm supposed to do, and then some. Sort of above and beyond. And I'm thinking, "Boy, would I have gotten away with that too?" I can never come up with "Yes". And I see that a lot, where minimal effort gets maximum reward in the end, and where maximum effort does not necessarily mean maximum reward.

Though primarily unconscious, and at times frustrating, these early incursions into administrative territory provided avenues for the aspiring assistant principals to reconnoitre the organizational landscape from their teaching positions and to improve their existing cognitive and social maps. These initial steps also allowed them to determine if administration was a desirable route, to evaluate their potential for success, and to prove that they were ready to become administrators. At the same time, these Entry-Exit rites also allowed their principals and superintendents to assess the administrative candidates' abilities. In turn, these supervisors rewarded some of the aspirants' perceived commitments to administration by acting as mentors and sponsors during the district selection and promotion rounds.

Selection, Promotion, and Placement

Administrative selection, promotion, and placement processes are an important part of organizational slotting and sorting mechanisms that allow senior officers to test administrative candidates' abilities to conform to the administrative culture. Although school district selection processes are generally governed by formal district policies and procedures, they may vary from district to district depending on the behaviors of senior administrators, as well as the prevailing political and organizational climate. In most jurisdictions, candidates complete written application forms, submit a leadership portfolio, and participate in structured interviews with senior administrators, which focus on their leadership skills and the resolution of a variety of case-based scenarios. Like the provincial certification process, the administrative candidates' school districts' selection and promotion procedures were outlined in policy and acted as an additional formal separation rite of passage. However, when compared with the provincial certification process, the district procedures were more consistent with previous descriptions of organizational socialization (see

Fishbein & Osterman, 2001; Greenfield, 1985a; Marshall, 1992a) and were experienced as unpredictable and disempowering.

The assistant principals described this phase of the cycle as diametrically opposed to the certification courses where they felt they could exercise some degree of control over events. As they progressed through the selection and placement process, the administrative candidates began to see a different perspective of the micropolitical structures that supported different career pathways. During this period, the administrative aspirants were required to undergo individual tests in order to prove to their supervisors that they possessed the knowledge and skills required to join the administrative group. This period of formal and informal testing required prospective candidates to interact directly with senior administrators whose behavior sent clear messages to the aspirants regarding the nature of organizational power dynamics and subordinate/superior relationships.

The assistant principals identified inconsistent practices and levels of support during their district's selection and placement process. Some of the candidates were also shocked to discover inequitable practices where candidates who had access to powerful networks received additional coaching, and were provided with sample interview questions. These included elite study groups which were set up by supervisory staff for specific individuals, structured programs for all administrative candidates, and informal meetings with administrative mentors and other teachers who were going through the process. For example, Karen, who worked closely with her administrative team, was invited to participate in a leadership study group that was convened by her area school superintendent and was coached throughout the interview process:

> We basically created our own PD. We did a session on how to deal with difficult situations. Also, during the promotion process, our family of schools had little sessions for those who actually put themselves through the rounds. They helped them through the interview process, we had mock interviews, we had sample questions, and we went through all these trials.

Although assistant principals like Barb, Karen, Sandy, Andrew, and Greg felt that they were supported by their supervisors to varying degrees, aspiring administrators who lacked administrative sponsors were unlikely to be successful in the district selection rounds, particularly if their application was not fully endorsed by their principal and/or supervisory officer. Consistent with her earlier observations, Sandy commented:

> I've said to one particular friend, "I feel I have been supported, but not necessarily helped." And that's the big difference. And I will give you the specifics of that. I've been supported in the sense that I've been told, verbally, "You're wonderful! You're great! You're a good leader!" And certainly I have been supported because I have made it through. So obviously the right things were also said to those people who ultimately make the choice.

As she compared her experiences with other favored administrative candidates, Sandy continued:

> But I have also heard of other people who had very concrete help. Like, they got calls from their superintendents, their principals, or what have you. They had mock interviews.

They had their resumes perused, and not necessarily because they ran after them [the senior officers], but they were solicited. I haven't gotten those. I remember in my particular case I even sent in my resume because there was an invitation sent out, and I never got any feedback. Or my principal, I think he was out of the office and sent an email, "Oh, by the way, do you have your resume? Do you want me to look at it?" Well it was due in about two hours. You know, stuff like that. So that's what I mean. Yeah, I have been supported. But did I get any specific help, sort of from the immediate people around me? No!

Candidates like Esther and Jerry who openly challenge administrative practices and lack powerful networks tell a different story. Even though they may meet the articulated certification criteria, they are likely to receive strong signals from their supervisors, which discourage them from applying for promotion. Those who persist, in spite of these messages, are usually "cut" in the interview rounds. Their experiences cohere with Greenfield's (1985a) observation that the relationship between supervisors and supervisees is not "affectively neutral" and that supervisors use their power to determine which candidates are selected. He points out that:

Subordinates who disagree with, threaten, or otherwise fail to act in a manner that is viewed as "acceptable" by superiors or sponsors risk the possibility, indeed a high probability, that their career aspirations may be stymied if not blocked or altogether redirected....Failure to demonstrate allegiance to the norms and values of the administrative group is likely to block the possibility of making the transition across inclusionary boundaries differentiating group members from non-group members, and central group members from members on the periphery. (p. 105)

Esther's story is illustrative of the insidious ways in which a district's supervisors use promotion processes to exclude or block the entry pathway to administrative candidates who do not support district administrative norms and beliefs. She identified her "stumbling blocks" as beginning when she applied for department headship against her principal's advice:

When the position came up...the principal decided, "No, I am not going to put you in this position." Mainly again, it is because I am an African Canadian...So she went out and she got a brand new person...who had been teaching for only two years...It was painful and upsetting because everyone knew that I could do the job...That was where the barriers started, where she decided that she did not want me to become an administrator.

Esther transferred to another school in order to avoid a confrontation with this principal which might impact her chances of promotion negatively. However, she was surprised to learn that even though she was told that she was successful in the interview, her former principal still had the power to prevent her name from being added to the district promotion list:

When I did my first interview, one of the principals who interviewed me, and he was not allowed to tell me this, but he said to me, "You did such an outstanding job that the people on the committee cannot believe that you are not already a vice-principal." When the superintendent went to the principal that did not give me the headship position, she said that she did not think I was ready and right there I was cut again...I went for the interview three times and each time she blocked me.

It was only after Esther appealed to another superintendent that she was placed on the official promotion list. Although Esther felt vindicated by the news of her promotion, she continued to voice her concerns:

> And after that, even after I got on the list, I realized that it is still who you know up at the top. If the principal who is working at the school where you are going to be placed doesn't really know you, or knows somebody who knows you, the chances of you getting on are very slim. There were two of us from my school board on the list. And I was selected mainly because somebody knows me and knows that I have done a lot of work in the community, and knows this neighborhood and my experience has spoken for me. But, had it not been for that, I probably would not have been selected.

While acknowledging that she herself has benefited from her contacts, she was disenchanted by cronyism on the part of senior officers who contradicted her district's espoused commitment to equitable hiring practices.

The assistant principals' experiences confirm Marshall's (1985a) findings that prospective assistant principals assess the value of the targeted career against other choices and the potential degree of difficulty in acquiring the stated and unstated qualifications. In addition to looking at career stereotypes, mentors, and sponsors and seeking access to formal and informal opportunities for training, they are also encouraged by a "tap on the shoulder" by their superiors. These early experiences can be a hindrance to new administrators' ability to cultivate innovative leadership responses if the types of role models they emulate only serve to reproduce custodial roles that reinforce systemic inequities.

Betwixt and Between

Although some of the assistant principals experienced ambiguous reactions to their promotion, positive feelings of pleasure, euphoria, and excitement dominated. All of the candidates were elated when they received news that they were going to be promoted. Their feelings of elation stemmed from the satisfaction of having accomplished their goal and the anticipation of the forthcoming upward change in their career pathway. Sandy also connected these feelings to the confirmation from her supervisors that her leadership skills had been recognized. She reminisced, "I was quite excited about it. And I guess I felt that a lot of the hard work I did had been rewarded...that a lot of my potential had been recognized." Recalling her excitement and relief when she learned that she was successful in the interview rounds, Karen remarked "I thought it was great. I was ecstatic." However, for Esther and Gerry who had been rejected multiple times, the excitement and relief of achieving their goal was clouded by feelings of disillusionment at what they considered to be a flawed selection process. Describing the news of her promotion as "bitter-sweet," Esther wondered aloud, "It was nice, but why should I be excited?" As she reflected on the sociopolitical landscape of her school district, she observed, "It's just a networking issue, and who you know and I don't even know if the best people make it all the time."

After their names were placed on the promotion list, the administrative candidates experienced varying waiting periods before the promotion list was officially published and before their school superintendents informed them that they were assigned to a new school. At this stage of the pathway, the administrative candidates were subjected to additional threshold rites. In addition to demonstrating patience with the process and trust in their supervisory officer, they were required to maintain periods of secrecy about their placement until the school board's official announcement. The assistant principals reported that colleagues who violated these secrecy rites were perceived as untrustworthy, and, in some cases, were punished by having their placement changed or rescinded.

Overall, these threshold experiences generated mixed feelings, which fluctuated between euphoria, fear, confusion, and self-doubt. For some candidates, the sense of accomplishment that they experienced on receiving news of their promotion was diminished by unconfirmed rumors, threats of sanctions from supervisors, and poor central office communication. Karen's initial excitement at the prospect of becoming an assistant principal was replaced by feelings of confusion and insecurity when her name did not appear on the promotion list which was publicly released. This was further exacerbated by her superintendent's refusal to provide her with written proof that she had been promoted. When her superintendent finally confirmed that she had been placed in a school and she shared the news with her family, friends, and colleagues he called to warn her not to discuss it any further. She recalled:

> I thought it was great. I was ecstatic. I was sitting here all evening waiting for the phone call because I knew what was happening. That feeling stayed for a few days until I got the other phone call that I was not supposed to tell anyone because the other family of schools hadn't mentioned it. That's when I started getting confused about not knowing the process. I was promoted in May and I was supposed to be introduced to the staff at the new school at their final staff meeting in June, but the teachers here didn't know about it until it was announced at the September staff meeting. Again it was the communication and I was a little bit confused. What am I allowed to say? What am I not allowed to say? Does that happen to anyone else?

Although Karen wondered if her experience was unique, other assistant principals' stories confirmed that this was not an anomaly. Michael, who perceived himself as emotionally stable was also surprised at the impact of the process and he described his journey as "a roller coaster of emotions – from anxiety to jubilation to relief." Having committed to the administrative pathway, he experienced "getting on the list" as an important milestone, and he reported doing a "happy dance" when he received the news. His euphoria was short-lived when he discovered that his name was omitted from the published list. After meeting with his supervisory officer, he was informed a week later that he had been placed in a new school:

> The superintendent calls me, she says, "I've got some news for you. You've been placed." I said, "I have?" I said, "I just talked to you last week or whatever." She said, "Yes, I know." You've been placed somewhere else and I can't tell you the details because everything is hush–hush. And I said, "Great, I'll look forward to getting a call from another superintendent."

His frustration and anxiety were increased during the ensuing waiting period because of his inability to get concrete information from central office about his new school and unwritten administrative protocols which prevented him from contacting his new principal directly:

> So there was a lot of anxiety, like, "What am I supposed to do?" And I hadn't got any information about the school. You know, I went on the web and checked the website, and looked up Board publications to find out a little bit. The website told me about administrators that hadn't been here for about eight months before... And then the anxiety passed a little bit and it became back to, "Oh, I'd like to get started." And it was, "I want to get in the school." But there is no opportunity to get in the school.

The administrative candidates' success in their district's selection, promotion, and placement rounds also placed them in an ambiguous relationship between teachers and administrators. This may be attributed to the fact that Exit and Entry are co-occurring cycles which require individuals to leave teacher territory while attempting to break administrative ground. While these aspiring administrators had recognized this at a surface level, they were unprepared for the deep emotions that were evoked when they realized the ramifications of their decision. The aspirants' early orientation rites signaled their intentions to the administrative corps, and for the most part, they were encouraged by practising administrators who facilitated movement along the promotion pathway. However, these social and psychological forays into administrative territory (GASing) also inadvertently communicated the administrative candidates' desire to separate from teaching. Perceiving their colleagues' shift in allegiance as an attempt to break ranks, some of the veteran teachers experienced it as a threat to the solidarity of the teacher group and in some cases they accused them of "climbing the ranks" or "selling out."

The combination of feelings of powerlessness, fear of sanctions from senior officials, and negative pressure from their teaching colleagues introduces an element of instability to this first epicycle and administrative candidates experienced feelings of guilt and self-doubt. This range of mixed emotions during this first cycle is also consistent with previous descriptions of the liminal (intermediate) nature of change and transitional phenomena (Bridges, 2003; Dotlich et al., 2004; Sigford, 1998). Trice and Morand (1989) describe liminality as:

> [A] state of limbo in which the newcomer is marginal, experiencing a state of not being in his or her old role, or, for that matter, in the one toward which the passage is leading him or her. It is an unstructured and ambiguous state of "betwixt-and-between". (p. 400)

The aspiring assistant principals responded to the dissonance of the Entry–Exit cycle by attempting to straddle both teaching and administrative territory. Moving back and forth between what was sometimes experienced as opposing worlds led to the development of a bifocal perspective, which allowed them to see both teaching and administrative points of view. In Karen's situation, her dual roles as a teacher union representative and future administrator placed her in a difficult middle location, where she felt that she could understand "both sides" of the negotiation issues between teachers and the school district:

And you sort of see both sides now and you know your duty is towards the teachers and helping them out. But then, on the other hand, you see how administrators are thinking. ... So I was caught between the two.

However, the pressure of identifying with both groups led to emotional ambiguity, and this dual allegiance became a growing source of internal conflict as she attempted to find neutral ground.

Leave Taking

As the prospective assistant principals' came closer to their official moving date, they were required to undergo additional teaching and administrative entry rites. During this period, they were invited to various functions at the school and district levels where they were introduced to, and welcomed by, their new staff. At the same time, they experienced mixed emotions as they participated in formal and informal farewell ceremonies with students and departmental colleagues and packed their boxes. In Michael's case, shifting between different groups and locations provoked emotional swings that were typified by happiness and sadness as he anticipated moving on:

People asked me, "Are you sad to be leaving your school?" "No, it's just something to do." And then, as I get closer, "Well, are you looking forward to it?" "Well, yes, I am looking forward to it, but I love what I am doing. So that's not a problem." But then, I really want to get in there. I really want to get started and I am sad to leave my school.

These co-occurring entry and exit rituals also triggered organizational divestiture and investiture rituals, which pressured the newly appointed assistant principals to shed their familiar teacher attachments and assume signifiers that were consistent with administrative status. Divestiture rites involved giving up such aspects of teaching, such as, leaving their former teacher roles, relationships, and locations, and they triggered feelings of sadness and trepidation. Greg recalled a sense of finality and sadness as he contemplated the prospect of leaving a successful teaching career behind and carving out a new pathway:

Incredible trepidation, hesitation, a great sense of loss, and a sense that I could not turn back to what I felt was the most ideal job I had ever had in my teaching career. So there was this grieving associated with that, more so than embracing a new position.

Investiture rites entailed receiving administrative rights and privileges that reinforced their new status. While most of the appointments were announced in the spring and the assistant principals did not officially begin duties until September, the new assistant principals were expected to help out during the summer in order to get set up for the coming school year. As the beginning of the school year approached, they were accorded administrative privileges and territorial rights, such as their own secretaries, offices, parking spaces, computers, walkie-talkies, security codes, and the keys to the building. While these visible and invisible markers reinforced their upward mobility, administrative status, and earlier feelings of accomplishment, they also confirmed their increasing distance from the teaching landscape.

The insecurity that then surfaced as a result of the realization that they were on foreign territory, and the lack of a conceptual map of this new administrative terrain, magnified their earlier feelings of trepidation and insecurity and provoked a crisis of meaning. Like Greg, Andrew experienced mixed emotions as he was struck by the irrevocability of his decision and realized that he could not go back. As he exited the teacher landscape, he also questioned the wisdom of the decision to leave a successful teaching career and he wondered whether he was moving in the right direction:

> And also at that time I remember feeling quite sad that I was leaving that school that I was in, leaving my school behind, leaving my department behind.... So I really felt that I left my department behind and definitely the kids. I really, really missed the kids. At that time I really questioned, should I or should I not? But I knew that once you've been appointed, you have to move forward.

Dealing with the simultaneous paradoxes of this physical, social, and psychological entry and exit process and the cumulative socialization challenges of the promotion process provoked feelings of disorientation and dislocation and moved the new administrators forward into the second epicycle of Immersion-Emersion, which is discussed in Chapter 6.

Chapter 6
Immersion–Emmersion: Ascending the Administrative Hierarchy

Abstract Chapter 6 explores the second epicycle of Immersion–Emersion where assistant principals come face to face with external school and district socialization demands. This period of shocks, surprises, and "absurd contrasts" is exacerbated by the ill-defined nature of the role of the assistant principal. This chapter describes the paradoxes and aporias that emanate from the assistant principals' social and psychological "middle space" location within the organizational hierarchy and their efforts to make sense of these early tensions and ambiguities.

The second epicycle of the assistant principals' trajectory occurred shortly after they left teaching and were physically located in their new schools. While the first cycle of Entry–Exit allowed for a gradual preview of the boundaries of the administrative terrain, Immersion–Emersion was experienced as a sudden shift that stripped the newly appointed assistant principals of their familiar teacher roles and contexts and immersed them in the middle of a different school culture. The assistant principals were almost immediately placed at the frontline of the school and were required to assume responsibility for a wide variety of duties and problems for which they had no prior preparation. In their location at the hub of school activity, they were inundated by unaccustomed pressures from students, parents, staff, district supervisors, and the external community, and pressured to provide quick solutions. This frequently conflicting range of demands and socializing forces and the abrupt shift in duties and physical locations created a sense of altered reality, as well as feelings of dislocation and disequilibrium.

Administrative Shocks and Surprises

The Immersion–Emersion cycle represented an intermediary period of emotional and cognitive upheaval because of concurrent changes in the assistant principals' personal, professional, and organizational contexts. Crossing the administrative threshold also exposed the new assistant principals to a different organizational perspective, and they were surprised to discover that the cognitive maps that they had developed during the first cycle from their teacher vantage point did not reflect their new location at the epicenter of the school community. In spite of the fact that the assistant principals were experienced teachers who had worked in a variety of school settings, this view of the organizational landscape was startling in its depth and complexity and it led to feelings of dislocation and disequilibrium.

The Immersion–Emersion period marked the first time in their career that the new administrators had to deal with school-wide concerns. The contrast between their previous focus on individual students and classes and the aggregate perspective of the school provoked cognitive and emotional dilemmas. The assistant principals' elevation within the administrative hierarchy also uncovered a complex web of social and political undercurrents that pervaded the educational landscape, but were previously not visible from their classroom location. Proximity to management issues, staff and student supervision, and chronic problems such as abuse, drugs, poverty, and racism opened their eyes to the ways in which institutional policies and procedures maintain societal inequities.

The assistant principals used a number of different metaphors to describe the intensity of this administrative shift. Assistant principals, particularly those who were promoted after the school year began, reported feeling as if they had "hit the ground running," and they were shocked by the almost immediate expectation that they should solve difficult problems without prior training. Andrew's metaphor of a time conversion tunnel illustrates the dynamics of the role propulsion which characterizes this cycle of the administrative passage:

> In June you were a teacher and you come here in September and all of a sudden you are not a teacher. You don't feel like a VP, but all these people think you can do all these things. They expect you to, as if you have passed through a tunnel and that tunnel converts you from a teacher to an administrator in that very short walk in the summer. And boom! You see the light.

Michael's image of a tornado also provides insight into the speed and vertigo of the second cycle and the feelings of instability and disequilibrium that accompanied the shift in roles and locations:

> For some reason, tornado comes to mind. That's the way it started. You get caught up and the next thing you know you are in this position. And everything is flying at you, and you have to learn everything all at once, and you turn this way, and that way, and the next way.

Frequent comparisons of their early months in the role as "a roller coaster of emotions," "a nightmare," "being in a spin," and "a sense of chaos" captured the shocks and surprises of the Immersion–Emersion epicycle and its pervasive impact. Similarly, metaphors such as "jumping off the deep end" and "swimming against the tide" speak to the difficulty of the immersive socialization processes and the dislocation and disequilibrium they provoked.

The assistant principals' responses are consistent with previous observations that shocks, surprises, and contrasts are universal phenomena that accompany transition and socialization processes (Brammer, 1991; Cantwell, 1993; Hartzell et al., 1994; Marshall, 1985a; Nicholson & West, 1988). Louis (1980) describes the cognitive impact of this physical and social shift:

At that particular time, all surroundings, that is, the entire organizationally-based physical and social world, are changed. There is no gradual exposure and no real way to confront the situation a little at a time. Rather, the newcomer's senses are simultaneously inundated with many unfamiliar cues. (p. 230)

Although their promotion had confirmed their official entry into the administrative passage, the new assistant principals were still vested in their teaching role and identity, and moving to the second level of their administrative trajectory was experienced as a form of culture shock. Schmidt (2000) connects new school administrators' feelings of culture shock to the fact that teachers carry a latent cultural membership or reference group orientation with them when they assume administrative roles. Ingrained aspects of their teaching culture influence their attitudes, behaviors, and emotions and may increase feelings of role strain during this transition period. Hartzell et al. (1994) also attribute the phenomenon of surprise to individual, contextual, and role variables, and they hypothesize that teachers who become administrators have difficulty anticipating transitional changes because they still remain in the field of education and in schools, their initial and at this point, primary professional reference points.

Middle Space and Absurd Contrasts

A large part of the shocks and surprises of the Immersion–Emersion cycle can also be attributed to the liminal or in-between psychological state that accompanies role transitions and passages and ambiguities that characterize the assistant principals' role and organizational location. Bernard Oshry's (1993) notion of "middle space" provides a useful metaphor for understanding some of the psychological and social phenomena that emerged during the new assistant principals' early role transition. Although Oshry does not use this term with reference to the assistant principalship or transitional epicycles, it can be extended to improve our understanding of the assistant principals' social and emotional location within the Immersion–Emersion cycle, and the ambiguities that arise out of this middle-management role (Armstrong, 2005). The concept of "middle space" is also consistent with the "betwixt and between" or liminal feelings of disequilibrium and dislocation that characterize transitional neutral zones and passages (Bridges, 2001; Marris, 1974; Van Gennep, 1960) and aporia (Burbules, 1997).

Oshry describes middle space as the middle managers' location within the organizational hierarchy and their tendency to be "caught between the conflicting agendas, perspectives, priorities, needs, and demands of two or more individuals or groups" (p. 402). Oshry's characterization of managerial middle work as hectic, varied, fragmented, and disempowering coheres with the assistant principals' experiences. The assistant principalship is an amorphous management role which is sandwiched in the middle of senior management and other employee groups and at the beginning of the administrative hierarchy (Armstrong, 2005). Novice administrators experience this role as an ambiguous middle space, and they have difficulty understanding their location as a linkage between multiple stakeholders (see Fig. 4.1). The lack of clearly defined goals, boundaries, and duties increases transitional stress, strain, and confusion (Hartzell, 1991, 1993; Hartzell et al., 1994; Marshall, 1992a, 1992b).

The assistant principals identified achieving a clear sense of the expectations and boundaries of their role as difficult because of the number of disconnected roles and duties they had to assume, the lack of time and space to monitor results, and the fragmented emotions it evoked. Commenting on the diffuse nature of the assistant principal role, Barb observed:

> And know that your job is anything. There is no job description. It is duties as assigned by the principal, which means your job is anything. And your job does not stop at the end of June and start at the beginning of September. So if you are not ready to commit a portion of your life, it is not easy.

Assistant principal Greg used the term "absurd contrasts" to describe the paradoxes and tensions that new assistant principals experience as they attempt to make sense of the contradictions between the reality of the assistant principal's role and their pre-role expectations. Although these paradoxes are normally embedded within administrative roles and organizational power dynamics, they become more disturbing when new assistant principals see them through their latent teachers' lenses. These contradictions create additional disjunctions when the newcomers' pre-role expectations collide with the on-the-ground realities of their managerial middle space and the surrounding socialization context.

The new assistant principals experienced absurd contrasts during the Immersion–Emmersion period because of their psychological connection with their former teaching culture and their lack of preparation for assistant principal roles. As former teachers, who were accustomed to the relative anonymity, regularity, and structure of the classroom, they experienced a high degree of dissonance when they were promoted to an unclear location at the very center of school activity. Greg's depiction of the assistant principalship as an entity which is greater than the sum of its parts illustrates the diffuse and precarious nature of the assistant principal's limited power to influence events, when contrasted with its diverse range of responsibilities:

> As a vice-principal, you are really at the epicenter of all of those structures – societal, familial, organizational, and financial. So you are more than yourself because you have a vital connection to all of those and you are really at the center of that. You are more than who you are because you have a position of great responsibility. You are trusted with the well-being of all of those children. You are also trusted by the Ministry and the Board to carry out their mandate. You could be stripped of that very, very quickly as soon as you do anything that any one of those other spokes feels is incorrect. You are more than who you are. That you are less than who you are is also true.

This analysis of the assistant principalship goes to the core of the ambiguities which the newcomers face as they enter this unstable political and social location. New assistant principals feel overwhelmed by the legal and moral complexity of their role, and their transitional stress is further increased by the wide range of socialization forces which impact their role.

Immersion Rites – Separation, Isolation, and Intimidation

The Immersion–Emersion cycle placed the new assistant principals in a challenging middle space between two competing professional landscapes, and it triggered hidden organizational dynamics which normally protect teaching and administrative territory and regulate the passage between these teaching and administrative roles (Armstrong, in press-b). During this cycle, the assistant principals experienced an intensification of the Entry–Exit threshold rites which attempted to separate them from teaching and to inculcate administrative norms and roles. Their descriptions of immersion socialization tactics are consistent with grinding down processes (Van Gennep, 1960), which test the newcomers physically, socially, and psychologically by subjecting them to difficult conditions and tasks (Armstrong, in press-b). Sandy's fire-and-water imagery attests to the shock of the early immersion period and the lack of training and support the assistant principals received:

> It is really, you drop in the pool and you sink or you swim, trial by fire, to put out all the clichés. It is a job where you learn by doing. Sometimes you have the opportunity to get some practice and exposure, but not a great deal.

These immersion rites contributed additional aporias during their first few months on the job as the assistant principals attempted to negotiate unfamiliar administrative terrain, tasks, and systems with limited role and organizational road maps.

The assistant principals had also entered the administrative pathway believing that it would lead to transformative leadership work on their part because this notion was reinforced in their professional certification courses and in their district's promotion criteria. They were therefore surprised by the almost immediate rejection of their curricular expertise and the almost unilateral expectation from the school community that they dress, speak, and behave like "administrators" and fulfil managerial and disciplinary roles. Students, parents, and staff emphasized the newcomers' transitional status, and they communicated messages regarding appropriate physical and professional domains, as well as social and professional boundaries. Assistant principals who transgressed these boundaries were subjected to subtle pressure or overt reprimands. Greg described how community socializing pressures imposed narrow role parameters on newcomers and constrained their early attempts to resist these traditional and custodial role orientations:

> People expect you to change because if you are on a stage, you are now in the role of vice-principal, everybody has a particular definition of what that role and what that script is, and if you are not going according to the script, people remind you. They put you in your place, whether it's a student, a parent, the way you dress, the fact that you have an office. All of those things redefine you, whether you like it or not.

In spite of the fact that the assistant principals' days were consumed by student-related issues, they described their interactions with adults as the most stressful part of their job. They were surprised by the wide range of demands and the lack of respect from some of the parents, teachers, and district office staff. Assistant principals like Greg, who previously worked in less-advantaged schools, expressed

concern regarding the ways in which some of the richer parents used their political
and legal power to subvert rules and override decisions by assistant principals:

> In this neighborhood, the biggest surprise is the amount of time, resources and energy that
> the parents put into treating the public system as a private school for their own children. The
> parents are very demanding and sometimes they don't have a right to be that demanding
> given the resources we don't have. They try to intimidate.

Although the assistant principals had anticipated some changes between teaching and administrative duties, they were surprised by the extensive pressure that was
used in order to separate them from teachers and teaching-related functions. They
were discouraged from visiting areas such as the staffroom or classrooms, which
were designated as teacher territory. Sandy observed, "It's geographical, you know,
there's the classroom and there's the office, and the halls. These are my domains
now, the office and the halls, and the doorways of classrooms when they are open."
This narrow delineation of physical and social boundaries further reduced the newcomers' sphere of interaction and increased their feelings of loss and isolation.
This practice is consistent with previous studies which point to the existence of
teacher and administrative dynamics that maintain separate teacher and administrative groups and pressure new assistant principals to distance themselves from
teachers and teacher roles (Sigford, 1998). Conway (1990) confirms the existence
of separation rites that reinforce differences between teachers and administrators,
and underscore a "we versus they" mentality (p. 198). Matthews and Crow (2003)
also observe that:

> Teachers, in order to maintain the teacher subculture, try to keep the division of authority
> and lines of communication clear. Administrators, sometimes in response to this subculture,
> attempt to close ranks and create an "us and them" perspective in new assistant principals.
> (p. 277)

The abrupt nature of the change in relationships with their teaching colleagues
was a shock for the new assistant principals, who still identified with the teaching
corps. They were also surprised by the tactics which some of the veteran teachers
used to intimidate and/or humiliate them. In many instances, veteran teachers
attempted to destabilize the novices by discounting their suggestions and by-passing
their authority by going directly to their principals. Even more surprising was the
fact that their principals sometimes colluded with the teachers. Karen described how
her confidence was undermined when veteran teachers questioned her directly about
her lack of prior administrative experience: "And it just threw me off. They didn't
think I was good enough and I had to work at proving myself in the school." Andrew
also reported instances of bullying and intimidation: "Some could be quite aggres-
sive and challenge you because you are an administrator. They try to put you on the
spot, just to test you. Some teachers. . .actually went to the point of being rude."

The assistant principals were also surprised to find that, while the teaching faculty no longer respected their curriculum expertise, they expected them to resolve
a number of issues. The unrealistic level of teacher expectations and the range and
depth of the problems the assistant principals were expected to solve contributed
additional pressure. Esther observed:

I am surprised at how much teachers look to you, and expect you to know the job and respond appropriately. And without preparation, practice, and experience, you could find yourself in deep waters. But that is something that new VPs have not been exposed to. You need that kind of training and time too. They really expect you to give the right answers and to be knowledgeable.

The assistant principals were also subjected to "sink or swim" initiation rites by members of their own administrative team who assigned them difficult and time-consuming tasks related to technical and data management, large-scale decision making, timetabling, and discipline management, while withholding training and critical pieces of information. During this early induction phase, the new adminis-trators were provided with a list of their duties which described their general areas of responsibility. There was no prior consultation, their responsibilities were not matched to their strengths, and most of them were unable to meet with their prede-cessors, who had already moved on to other schools. Reflecting on her introduction to the role, Sandy acknowledged:

I had no idea of the job. I just made up what I am supposed to do. When I came, it was all operational things. I had the same piece of paper that my predecessor had. I was in charge of exams, I was in charge of this and that. That's not a job description, it's a duties list. That's all I got.

Furthermore, although they were expected to manage the complex student and staff information systems, the assistant principals received little or no basic techni-cal training in areas which were integral to their role performance, such as student registration and scheduling. As she described her first few weeks, Barb identified adjusting to unstructured days and reacting to the wide variety of tasks and con-stituent demands as key challenges:

At the beginning, you think. "I don't have anywhere to go." I don't have anything to do. What's my day going to look like? You know, you've been teaching and everything's planned out for you and you know that on the bell you know you have to be somewhere else and you know that these are the kids that you are going to see....And then all of a sudden, your day becomes incredibly full. Am I dealing with this kid? Should I take this phone call? I need to be up in this classroom. What's the most important thing to do at the time? How do I use this computer system? How do I search for a student?

This lack of support magnified their early aporias, led to feelings of incompe-tence, and forced the assistant principals to rely on veteran administrators. Andrew described his early feelings of inadequacy, "I remember the first several weeks that feeling of inadequacy really puts you down. You don't know if you should ask this person or that. There was no training." Their attempts to train themselves after school led to longer workdays that increased their physical and mental strain. Esther observed:

I have to stay behind to train myself. I have to ask people. But the student information system is very important in that you need to know right away. I asked them to put me on, but I have not been given formal training in it....So I find it is slowing me down a little. But I am coping in the sense that I am putting in a lot of hours at the end of the day. I have been here until 8:30 at night...sometimes 9:00.

In more extreme cases, degradation rites were used to demoralize the new assistant principals and ensure compliance. Jerry's transition to a large urban school was further exacerbated by his principal's command-control tactics. These involved denial of common administrative privileges, such as purchasing cards and master keys, prohibition from socializing with teachers, and frequent and unexpected humiliations in public. Jerry became emotional as he described the humiliation and powerlessness he felt as his decisions were undermined by his principal:

> Not being given respect that you have the ability to make decisions... having your decisions overturned in your face in front of students and staff... being treated like you are two years old...Having someone [the principal] come into your office while you are dealing with parents and demanding that you come and do what she is dealing with. She would kick my butt every day. And being new and coming back into a big collegiate, I really got sort of lost.

However, in spite of his outrage at this violation of his employee rights, he was afraid of complaining to his superintendent because he no longer had the protection of a union. An additional source of fear was related to the knowledge that speaking out against his principal would be a "career limiting move," which could incur negative career repercussions and restrict his chances for promotion in the long-run.

The assistant principals also experienced pressure from senior management to implement policies and solve problems without the required training, support, or discretionary power. For the most part, these policies were created without prior consultation with school-level administrators and were communicated as top-down written directives. District policies also had the unintended effect of increasing power struggles between assistant principals and faculty, particularly when these directives contradicted local schools' values and priorities. Michael described a complex political dynamic, which entailed complying with external mandates and buffering students, while accommodating teacher resistance:

> Oftentimes we get a direction from the board to get this in place and the teachers are pushing back on the other side, and then the students get caught in the middle. So it is trying to work this out so that however we decide to implement the direction of the board, it is softened so that the teachers can get behind it and work toward some way of adopting it and helping the students to benefit from all of this.

The ever-present threat of teachers' grievances and union sanctions also exacerbated newcomers' fears and increased their sense of powerlessness. Commenting on the collective power of teachers, Sandy expressed her frustration at her inability to implement curriculum change on behalf of students. She wondered how this dynamic could be addressed:

> And how do you get around that? And you know the radicals will circle the moment it gets back. You know for sure that the way you deal with one teacher is known to all teachers, almost immediately. I guess it is a negative collegiality in certain ways, because they support each other. But often times, it is supporting in a way to fossilize even further those negative behaviors, or keep them in confrontation with students.

The pressure to execute their role in exactly the same way as their predecessors increased the newcomers' feelings of insecurity and forced them to rely on veterans and to commit to custodial management roles. Sandy observed, "When you are new at a job, you tend to follow the rules. You don't make your own interpretation, because you want to do things right." This combination of informal, random, and variable district socialization practices communicated contradictory messages to newcomers and increased their feelings of role ambiguity and strain.

Between Leadership and Management

Conflicts between the assistant principals' psychological location as teachers and the institutional pressure to assume custodial management roles also contributed to the absurd contrasts of the Immersion cycle. Although the new assistant principals assumed that their days would be spent on leadership initiatives that supported positive staff and student growth, the majority of their time and attention was consumed by supervisory and stabilizing roles related to plant, student, and staff supervision, and monitoring. As he contrasted his former teaching and current administrative roles, Andrew expressed regret at having chosen the administrative route:

> When you are in the classroom, you have the really bright ones and then those that need extra care. You have a range of different kids in terms of their ability. But in this job as a vice-principal, unfortunately, most of the time, we deal with students who need the extra care. So, at the end of the day, we are always looking at the school from the bad side. Or someone would also use the analogy of looking at it from the rear end. That's unpleasant, because it always sticks in your face.

The diffuse nature of their role also left the assistant principals open to unrealistic and sometimes competing expectations from sources both inside and outside of the school community. Assistant principals are pressured to be planners, problem solvers, mediators, and buffers between a wide range of organizational stakeholders inside and outside of their school. Karen described how solving other people's problems dominated the role:

> Problem solving is the single most important aspect of this job because that's what you are continuously being asked to do. You are presented with hundreds of different problems in any given day and it's the expectation that you are to solve the problem.

The assistant principals were also shocked when they were required almost immediately to resolve a diverse range of issues for which they had no training, including those related to verbal and physical conflicts, firearm and bomb threats, chemical leaks, drug abuse, and suicidal students. The unpredictability of these events and the enormous responsibility of making decisions in these high-risk situations exacerbated their feelings of vulnerability. Michael recalled his anxiety when he was forced to evacuate the school because the other administrators were away:

> So in the first week we had the bomb threat here. I knew what my responsibility was and I did it, but at the same time, I was nervous. It was the first crisis that I've ever had to start making decisions for.

The chronic nature of their community's problems and the crisis-filled nature of their role led to pervasive feelings of insecurity. Barb observed:

> When you start as a vice-principal often times you are dealing with the negative stuff, or the in your face stuff and there is not a lot of patting you on the back, but there are a lot of expectations that you'll solve the world's problems. And, I think that is probably what made me wonder if I was doing an OK job or if anybody knew that I was doing an OK job.

The lack of feedback and the absence of avenues to express their concerns intensified the administrators' feelings of powerlessness, and at times, they wondered if they had made the right career choice.

The assistant principals' fear of being perceived as incompetent was further exacerbated by their responsibility to maintain school safety. This aspect of their role heightened their anxieties, particularly when they were required to intervene in violent incidents. In many cases, the assistant principals related stories about administrators who were physically or verbally attacked, whose car tires were slashed, or whose offices were firebombed. Barb shuddered as she recalled an earlier confrontation with a student: "I remember when that boy came after me in the first year with the fists clenched and was about to attack me...." Concerns about their personal safety were also accompanied by the pervasive fear that they would fail to protect students and staff from the criminal elements who frequented their buildings. Although Michael was placed in a suburban middle class school, he experienced ongoing stress because of the security demands of his role:

> And often, when these violent incidents happen, always in the back of my mind is my safety and the students' safety, because you never know what these people are carrying anymore, if they have guns, knives, whatever. In this case, one of the assailants had a knife on them and they got rid of it.

In spite of these concerns, both male and female assistants were reluctant to discuss these issues with their teaching and administrative colleagues because of administrative taboos which prohibit demonstrations of fear (Marshall, 1985a). Andrew's reflection on his fears illustrates how assistant principals' passages are shaped by institutional narratives which construct assistant principals as "resident cops" and "problem solvers." He admitted quietly:

> Part of me felt really scared. And you can't tell anyone. You can't even go and tell the principal because you would not want to be seen as incompetent. You're a vice-principal now. You're no longer a teacher. You are now an administrator.

While hiding their fear developed stakeholder trust in their ability to handle crises, the assistant principals' silence unintentionally perpetuated the existing institutional metanarratives of the "fearless" assistant principal. These tacit arrangements also put them at risk both physically and emotionally, and ensured that endemic safety issues and their underlying causes remained unaddressed at the community level.

The assistant principals' disciplinary role was also narrowly circumscribed by the prevailing discourse of safe schools. The divergence between their expectations of their role as transformative leaders, and the staff's narrow perception of their function as disciplinarians and "enforcers," also constituted an ongoing source of stress and strain. Sandy expressed frustration at the fact that the assistant principalship is used as a "dumping ground" for the tasks that teachers and principals refuse to do:

> The vice-principal is perceived as the fixer of all things, is the axe that is going to get rid of the nuisance factor in the school and make life easier. That is a kind of a perception or a hope for you. And because of that, you are being judged according to how well you serve the expectations of teachers in taking care of their needs.

Disciplinary policies often created conflict between the assistant principals, students, teachers, parents, and other community groups because of the school district's demands. In many cases, the assistant principals questioned their role in implementing zero-tolerance policies which criminalized what they perceived to be "normal adolescent behaviors." The tension of disciplining and counseling students at the same time, attempting to please multiple constituents, and demonstrating competence, was described by Barb:

> Doing the other parts of my job that sometimes are on opposite poles – to advocate for students and to give out consequences. . .So that has been one thing, and it makes life difficult sometimes, because you always have to be on guard.

However, the assistant principals' early attempts to mitigate the negative impact of policies on poor, marginalized, and learning disabled students were often frustrated by entrenched teacher and administrative attitudes that pressured them to adopt tough disciplinary approaches. Esther's description of teacher intolerance illustrated the conflict between teacher and administrator perspectives on discipline. "Teachers think that students should be dealt with immediately, and perhaps harshly, at all times. We have to look at policy and where it fits." However, when confronted with disciplinary situations where they knew that teachers were wrong, the assistant principals sometimes succumbed to the teachers' demands because they were afraid of teacher grievances and union sanctions. The political and ethical tension involved in ensuring that students were dealt with fairly while at the same time not antagonizing teachers was captured in Sandy's admission:

> I have to be politically very astute here, but lots of times I do sympathize with those kids, to be very honest. And I do think they are telling the truth, so I do have to tread very carefully. Never undermine the teacher, never, never with them by saying, "You know, well actually, you're right and the teacher's wrong." You just never do that!

These external socializing pressures along with a difficult workload led to the development of punitive and reactive management styles. Greg expressed concerns about an emerging "knee-jerk management culture" which impacted students negatively:

> Most of the time we are reactive, so we tend to punish, and that does not have a long-range effect, so in fact, we are creating more problems in many cases by being reactive than proactive.

The contradiction between their desire to make a difference and their assumption of a punitive role which precluded opportunities for role innovation or transformative leadership prompted ethical conflict. As she reflected on her involvement in zero-tolerance practices, which she believed punished students unnecessarily and hindered their academic success, Esther questioned the true purposes of her role:

> Are we just there to take care of business or are we there to empower students, staff and community leaders? How can we can raise the academic level so that it can eventually spill over into society? How can we stop so many students being suspended and ending up in the court system? Many of them drop out of school and they do not become contributing members of society because they do not have an education.

An ongoing theme in the assistant principals' stories was related to the gap between their vast responsibilities and their limited institutional powers. As their first year progressed, the assistant principals experienced absurd contrasts when they compared their multiple accountabilities with the inability to control their role. Disjunctions between the assistant principals' pre-role assumptions about administrative power and the reality of their middle space role were illustrated in their stories of how their decisions were overturned by principals and/or superintendents because of complaints from parents or other stakeholders. Reflecting on her incoming illusion that she would have the power to effect positive change, Sandy laughed derisively at what she described as "the so-called power" of assistant principals:

> I think that's another perception that comes from people in the role. In the switch from teacher to vice-principal, maybe there is this perception. I think it is illusory that part of it is increased power.

Greg also contended that the assistant principalship was a role without substantive power since it was the repository for all of the jobs that the principal and the unionized staff refused to do:

> The only people who do not have a union and do not have any power, are the vice-principals. They can't say no. And so, what happens is, from both ends, a lot of the jobs that others can't do legitimately, somebody still has to do them. And so they end up on our laps and the laps of our secretaries.

He also challenged the myth that assistant principals were accorded a level of power commensurate with the importance of their position and responsibilities:

> You are under constant surveillance. You are constantly performing. But at the same time, it's all quite meaningless because you really don't have very much power when it comes right down to it. As a vice-principal, you really don't have much power. So it is this kind of absurd existence between those two – huge responsibility and perceived power. But by the same token, when you consider that everybody else has a huge chunk of you, you have nothing.

Michael's analogy of a magnifying glass also presented a compelling statement of the feelings of vulnerability which were provoked by his perceived lack of power:

> I feel helpless, because all you have to do is make a complaint to the top and people start putting a magnifying glass on you. And how many times do you need the magnifying glass on you? And then, when you are doing your day-to-day stuff, if you have to worry about a magnifying glass being put on you, how can you be effective there?

These disjunctions between real and perceived power, feelings of powerlessness, and the fear of external sanctions were strong socializing forces which restrict transformative leadership practices. For the most part, they motivated the assistant principals to opt for custodial roles, which in turn supported the more powerful interest groups and maintained the status quo.

Milestones and Anchors

In spite of these organizational socialization rites and restrictions, the second cycle of the assistant principals' trajectory was also punctuated by periods of emergence, where they attempted to resist the negative pull of the external socializing forces. While Immersion was characterized by feelings of inundation and a lack of control, Emersion was a complementary process of resurfacing which allowed the assistant principals to find identity moorings and to establish a firmer administrative footing. Assistant principals like Jerry, Greg, and Andrew, who determined that the role was untenable actively sought to return to teaching or to apply for leadership positions which they considered to be more consistent with their skills and values. However, they discovered that they had lost their teacher seniority due to their promotion to administration.

Increased familiarity with the role and its boundaries motivated the new assistant principals to move outward in order to find ways to reconcile personal and organizational expectations, and to find spaces where they could counteract the role's negativity. In order to resolve early aporias, Sandy frequently consulted with others and intentionally used her supervisory responsibilities as a way to meet staff and students and to escape the physical confines of her office:

> Part of it is because I did ask a lot of questions. I didn't feel that I was there alone. I asked a lot. I consulted a lot with my peers, my colleagues, be it the principal or the vice-principal. I made it a policy to go out and get to know the people in the school and I walked around.

Some of the administrators also attempted to establish more positive relationships with students and faculty by intentionally participating in co-curricular activities such as clubs and teams. Greg described being accepted as a coach by the students and teachers as an important turning point for him because it was seen as teacher territory:

> Like one thing I did this year which was important, here is a milestone. . ..I became a coach, and I co-coached the cross-country team, which meant being here early in the morning, running with the kids and going to a few meets. And then being enpowered to be away for a couple of days and telling everyone I won't be here because I've got another responsibility.

Contact with other administrators also helped to facilitate the Emersion period because of the support network that it provided. To a large extent, this entailed establishing support networks with others inside and outside of the school community for emotional and technical support. Like Karen, some of the other assistant principals renewed their earlier relationships with some of the teachers whom they had met during the Entry–Exit cycle, and who had also been promoted. She observed, "The other new administrators that I met through the principal's course and in the promotion process, we sort of still keep in touch. We still connect, a few of us, and we compare stories."

These small attempts at emergence allowed the assistant principals to develop a different perspective of their role and location, and helped to check the downward spiral of Immersion. However, the ongoing reactive and punitive nature of their role, the increasing disjunctions between their desired and enacted roles, and the persistent socialization pressure to conform to custodial roles, increased their feelings of frustration, loss, and anger, and precipitated the Disintegration–Reintegration cycle, which is discussed in Chapter 7.

Chapter 7
Disintegration–Reintegration: Shifting Perspectives – Letting Go, Holding On, and Reframing

Abstract Chapter 7 focuses on the third epicycle of the assistant principals' administrative passage. Disintegration–Reintegration is triggered by the ongoing conflict between the assistant principals' pre-role expectations and their external socialization challenges. In order to reconcile these tensions, the assistant principals adopted new schemas and dispositions which were more congruent with their administrative role demands. This entailed relinquishing some of their teaching skills and behaviors which were incompatible with their new role, as well as retaining and reframing their goals and values to make them more congruent with their emerging understanding of the administrative landscape.

The third epicycle of the assistant principals' administrative passage began during the latter part of their first year and lasted for most of their second year. This phase of role and perspective dissolution is provoked by the psychological dissonance of the transition itself and the ongoing socialization pressure to conform to institutional definitions of the assistant principalship. Disintegration, characterized by cognitive, emotional, and physical fatigue, and feelings of loss, isolation, and anger, requires the assistant principals to relinquish dysfunctional aspects of their role, while Reintegration entails reframing and retaining relevant skills and attitudes and finding alternative ways to enact their role. This involved acknowledging the limitations of their new role and discarding some of the pre-role behaviors and relationships that had contributed to their success as teachers, but which now conflicted with their community's expectations. It also entailed developing new relationships, skills, and competencies, as well as a more realistic outlook on their role and their place in the administrative hierarchy.

This process of letting go, holding on to, and reframing their pre-role behaviors and perspectives is consistent with resocialization, i.e., the ways in which role incumbents attempt to alter or replace dysfunctional roles (Fein, 1990). Bullogh et al.'s (1991) interpretation of Jean Piaget's process of assimilation and accommodation also provides insight into the social and psychological nature of Disintegration and Reintegration. They point out that:

> Assimilation refers to the process whereby objects and interactions are made meaningful through application of a schema without necessitating a stretching or adjusting of the

schema; the schema is fitting and the situation is thereby made sensible and more or less predictable. In contrast, accommodation refers to moments when schema necessarily must change in response to the inability to make a situation adequately and appropriately meaningful; that is, attending to a new situation necessitates a reorganization or a reconstruction of meanings in order to behave in ways that will achieve a desired end. (p.11)

For the assistant principals, accommodating and assimilating required developing new maps and schemas and reinterpreting their new knowledge and experiences to match these frameworks. These changes resulted in a paradigm shift, or fundamental changes in the individual's cognitive, emotional, and values structures. O'Connor and Wolfe (1991) describe this process as follows. "A new perspective is taken. There are new pieces to the puzzle, as well as new, creative re-arrangements of old pieces. One's constructions of reality are fundamentally different" (p. 326). The following sections describe the physical, social, and psychological factors that contributed to the assistant principals' shift in perspective.

Disintegration – Physical, Social, and Emotional Grinding Down

Disintegration was a process of role dissolution and divestiture, which was precipitated by the range and intensity of external demands and the pressure to perform a difficult and ambiguous role without adequate support. The assistant principals described long and unrelenting workdays which were characterized by disciplinary issues, problem solving, crisis management, frustration, and anxiety. In addition, persistent "grinding down" tactics, such as excessive workloads, exposure to endemic safety issues, responsibility to maintain safety in an unpredictable environment, and restricted avenues for expressing their fears and concerns led to cognitive, emotional, and physical strain and exhaustion. Adapting to the unrelenting pace of their role, responding to unreasonable and excessive demands and unanticipated crises, and providing quick solutions to complex issues provoked ethical tensions and feelings of incompetence. This was further compounded by feelings of overwhelming responsibility and powerlessness, the fear of being judged as incompetent, and a general lack of feedback.

In order to compensate for the lack of time during the school day, the assistant principals often spent their evenings at home or at work making phone calls to parents regarding student infractions, catching up with unfinished paperwork, or answering e-mails. As Karen described her resulting mental and physical fatigue, she observed,

There seemed to be a lot more of it and not enough time in the day. Things keep coming. During the day, I can't do my paperwork. I have to wait until after work. The paperwork and the time commitment seem to be increasing. You know, trying to stay on top of it. I'm usually in by 7:30 in the morning. I figure I'd get at least half an hour of quiet time before things start happening, and then I stay until 6 or 7.

The ongoing stress of reacting to multiple stakeholder demands and disciplinary issues also impacted their basic physical needs, such as eating and going to the washroom, and interrupted their sleep patterns. As the school year progressed, the cumulative effects of these external demands exacted a physical and psychological toll on the assistant principals. They identified developing physical ailments such as increased blood pressure, headaches, and fatigue which they connected to the physical and mental demands of their role.

Jerry reported elevated stress levels which also had a negative impact on his eating and exercise habits and his personal relationships. During one of our late afternoon conversations, he pointed to his lunch and remarked,

> My average day now, I come in and have a coffee in the morning. I bring my lunch because my wife is trying to make me healthy. Have I seen my lunch? No. It's there. Probably three to four days a week, I don't get to see my lunch until 4:30 or 5:00.

Although he was an avid sportsman who engaged in an active routine before his promotion, he found that his extended and unpredictable workday precluded him from going to the gym or participating in hockey games with his former teaching colleagues. His frustration with the constraints of the job and his lack of self-discipline resulted in feelings of self-blame and anger as expressed in the following comment:

> I'm just more on an edge. My friends notice it. My family notices it. I can no longer play hockey twice a week. I don't get to work out. I'm in the worst shape of my life. I have the worst diet of my life. I hate myself physically and emotionally because of that, because I have guilt from not working out. I just do. I can't get up any earlier and workout because I have to get here. I can't work out. It's just too hard for me. So I have guilt.

Andrew expressed similar feelings of self-reproach about his physical and emotional health and his personal relationships. Although he was grateful for his wife's assistance in picking up the extra chores and looking after their children, he was particularly worried about the impact of his long days on his family relationships. Additional concerns related to changes in his eating habits and exercise regime which were impacting his health negatively:

> I gained a few pounds because of a lack of exercise. That is very true and in fact the last couple of days I have been having very serious concern in terms of my personal health situation. ... And honestly that weight is not the consumption part, because unlike before when I was a teacher, we hardly have time for lunch.

The following excerpts from a conversation with Barb also illustrate the pervasive physical and psychological nature of the Disintegration cycle. As she reflected on the day-to-day challenges of her role and the shift in perspective that occurred when she became more integrated into her administrative role, she identified a pervasive obsession with operational and personnel issues. This was further exacerbated by feelings of powerlessness related to her commitment to address chronic issues such as poverty, which also impacted the well-being of her student body. She said,

> I probably eat, breathe and sleep my job more than I used to. At the end of the day, after teaching and coaching I would just drive home. There wasn't stuff that would eat at my soul. And here, I think that there is stuff that eats at my soul whether it's a very needy kid whose mom won't participate in his education, or whether it is, like today, a teacher who decides that he or she has a medical appointment at the 11th hour and I get an unforeseen

absence report two hours before the teacher is due to leave. And, I ask for lesson plans and all I am given is handouts, with no lesson plan. So this kind of stuff will eat at me on my way home... In the morning, when I do my teacher absences, I drive to school and I think, "I wonder if I have got someone in there?" So, I guess my school day starts from the time I wake up till the time I go to sleep, because there is always something that is going on in my brain about "What did I need to do? What could I have done better?" and that kind of stuff. So, you know, waking up in the middle of the night and jotting notes down.

The cumulative toll of her responsibilities, her concerns about social justice, and her inability to mitigate the effects of these issues increased her feelings of physical and psychological disintegration:

> Sometimes it is physically exhausting because stuff keeps coming at you. It is emotionally exhausting because, for a number of reasons, where these kids come from – often they are not well nourished, so you are feeling sorry for where they are coming from. It's taxing to your soul because of the struggles that the kids have on a daily basis. And just battling for them – being a voice for them out there in the community, out there with the government – just equity for these kids who haven't had much equity in their life.

Over time, these ongoing conflicts and dilemmas, combined with the realization that their teaching pathway was closed, pushed the assistant principals deeper into the Disintegration cycle, and they reported having to reach inward in order to determine how they could accommodate to their role.

Digging Deeper and Letting Go

The descriptions of Disintegration which emerged out of the assistant principals' stories provide insight into the complex and contradictory processes that are inherent in paradigm and perspective shifts and administrative passages. Felner, Farber, and Primavera (1983) and Marshall and Mitchell (1991) indicate that individuals facing changes have to reorder their "assumptive worlds." This encompasses their view of the world both as it is and as it might be. It includes interpersonal relationships, familiar environments, possessions, physical and mental capacities, roles, and statuses.

> From this perspective, when individuals face major life changes the key task they are confronted with is to modify their existing set of expectations and assumptions about their world and develop others which more accurately reflect their new situation. (Felner et al., 1983, p. 210)

Marris' (1974) research on loss and grieving also indicates that individuals go through a process of cognitive and emotional reorganization in order to reconcile their loss:

> When the loss is irretrievable, there must be a reinterpretation of what we have learned about our purposes and attachments – and the principles which underlie the regularity of experience – radical enough to trace out the thread again. ... The conservative impulse will

make us seek to deny the loss. But when this fails, it will also lead us to repair the thread, tying past, present and future together with rewoven strands of meaning. (p. 21)

As the school year progressed, the assistant principals reported undergoing a period of self-evaluation in order to reconcile the conflicts between the negative demands of their role and their own personal values and expectations. This entailed deconstructing their previous notions of the assistant principalship and consciously (or unconsciously) accepting that they would stay in the role in spite of its negativity, and finding meaning in their work. It also included seeking out ways to fit in, while circumventing or resisting the negative role pressures. Greg used the analogy of "digging deeper" to describe this inner shift, which entailed letting go of and/or reframing the outmoded skills, values, and attitudes and developing a new set of competencies that were more appropriate. Reflecting on this psychological process, he observed,

> What I am finding is that the talents that were being underutilized were not necessarily appropriate to the job, so I've had to mourn that loss. But, I've come to realize that there are other abilities that I have that I can put into place, that suit my personality. So it's been having to grudgingly give up some that were appropriate as a teacher, that may be appropriate in the position that I had before, and just mourn their loss. But, dig deep to find out what other aspects of my abilities can be brought into the job, to make it more than just a management position.

The process of letting go, holding on, and digging deeper gave rise to unexpected and painful emotional responses, such as feelings of loss, isolation, anger, and alienation. These emotions are consistent with previous reports that managers go through a grieving process when they attempt to reconcile their old and new perspectives and realities (Bridges, 1980, 2003; Dotlich et al., 2004). Hill's (1992) research on new managers identifies similar response patterns. She indicates, "A sense of isolation often follows a career transition. ... During times of transition, people feel lost as they find themselves without a clear reference group by which to identify appropriate values and norms" (p. 195).

Sigford's (1998) analysis of new school administrators' grieving processes also establishes a relationship between the level of disintegration experienced by novices, the function of the losses they experienced, and their coping skills. She indicates that bereavement follows when people leave meaningful work environments because their identity is tied up with their life circumstances, roles, and relationships. New administrators often see themselves and their transition in a new light as a result of the grief and bereavement process.

Although their promotion to administration was initially experienced as a gain, the newcomers' narratives showed that they had incurred a series of tangible and intangible losses. Tangible losses were easier to identify because they were related to the more visible aspects of the teaching environment such as familiar physical locations, schedules, teacher colleagues, and students. Although these were felt, their impact was not as sharp because the assistant principals had anticipated them in some measure. Intangible losses affected the assistant principals more deeply because these were connected to the assumptions, values, and perspectives at the core of their professional identities. Of particular concern to the assistant principals was the loss of their identity and role as curriculum leaders. As he reflected on the challenges of moving from a position of competence to incompetence, Greg described letting go of years of accumulated knowledge and experience as a difficult and emotional task:

> In terms of the challenge, there was embracing the new position. But as a curricular leader, as a teacher, that's what created a lot of loss. As an administrator, I am saddened that there are very few opportunities to be a curriculum leader. We are more reactive than active in this case.

Another key area of loss was related to their increasingly distant social and psychological connection to the teacher reference group. Although the assistant principals had taken their teaching status for granted, being a teacher also represented membership in the largest employee group in the school community and access to a vast support base. This social and emotional void was particularly unsettling to the assistant principals because of the dramatic reduction of their professional community, which was now limited to a handful of administrators with whom they were not always compatible. This loss of camaraderie and opportunity for collegial interaction was lamented by Sandy:

> You know, you come from a situation where you are interacting with a good number of colleagues. You know, you have sixty or whatever teachers in the school. You are not with all of them all the time, but you are interacting, especially if you have a pretty good rapport with people, which I did in the school. So that's a loss. So, sort of my peer community got reduced down to four.

As she reflected on the loneliness and isolation that accompanied the shift from being a member of a majority group (teachers) to becoming a member of a minority group (administrators), she acknowledged sadly, "You're no longer part of the inner circle. It's what they say. It's really lonely at the top."

The reduction in community and the loss of the relationships of trust they had built with teachers were particularly stressful for those assistant principals who were actively prevented from associating with the teaching staff, who did not get along with their administrative team, or who were placed in high-risk settings. In Jerry's case, finding appropriate social or emotional anchors within the confines of a toxic administrative team and a strong "us versus them" employee culture increased his feelings of loss:

> You are stuck with these four people in a bunker and there are bombs flying around overhead and you don't have much of a choice. You either get along right away to survive or you are gone. It's the old Bobby Knight army mentality where you hate the captain and so you sort of bond together because you have all this war going on and you have to survive.

This loss of collegial relationships with their teaching peers along with the sudden experience of being a minority exacerbated the assistant principals' feelings of marginalization and isolation. When combined with the external pressure to demonstrate administrative competence and the lack of recognition and support from their school district, these losses led to feelings of frustration, anger, and alienation.

Anger and Alienation

Sigford (1998) identifies anger as an important part of the process of loss and bereavement and she indicates that it may be used to mask the fear and sadness that new administrators are experiencing. Spector and Fox (2002) indicate that employees also experience anger and disengagement when they believe that the contracts, commitments, and obligations that exist between them and their employers are not being honored. Contracts relate to what is expected to be given to the employer (e.g., attendance and specific task performance) and what is received in return (e.g., benefits and salary). Although employer/employee commitments are often configured as legal contracts which articulate formal agreements, they also operate on the social and psychological levels. They can involve treatment and work assignments, as well as informal understandings and working norms, such as respect and reasonable working conditions which are critical to individual well-being and organizational success (Fineman et al., 2005).

A large part of the assistant principals' feelings of anger was related to the perception that their school district had violated its psychological contract with them. These feelings became more intensified when they realized that they could not return to teaching and were often directed toward their central office supervisors, whom the assistants believed were insensitive to their workloads and working conditions. As their school year progressed, they expressed a loss of faith in their employer because of its failure to provide training and working conditions which were comparable to those in teaching or the business industry.

As he compared the relative benefits of being a teacher and an administrator, Andrew highlighted a number of discrepancies related to working conditions and remuneration. In spite of his expressed decision to "stay in the role for the time being," he remained incensed at the school district's lack of commitment to assistant principals relative to teachers:

> I don't think that we are appreciated. We don't even have the same rights as a teacher. We don't even have anything in our contract. Our holidays are less. Our working hours are longer. In fact, our pay, when you look at our load, is less than the teachers'. So, you really wonder, "Am I crazy or what?" So, it's really an ironic situation even for someone from my background coming from the industry. I believe that a lot more could be done in the human resource area to address the situation with administrators if they want a sound system. So I think that is the discouraging part of being an administrator at this time, particularly in this school district.

When their school district cut back on hall monitors and supervisory duties were written out of the teachers' contract, these duties were also shifted to the assistant principals. The diminished support from the central office was most acutely felt by the assistant principals who were located in the more challenging schools because it added additional burdens to their already overcrowded schedules. Although the assistant principals supported the importance of maintaining safe schools, they believed these impositions to be indicative of senior officials' lack of respect and understanding of their plight. Jerry, who was placed in a large school with multiple safety challenges, was overwhelmed by his responsibility to supervise an extensive physical plant. After the school district took away one of the assistant principals and reduced their complement of hall monitors, he questioned angrily, "How do you take the most inner city school in the city, increase it by 300, and then take away 25% of the support staff in terms of the vice-principal and the hall monitors?"

His frustration at what he described as "one-size-fits all" policies and his concerns about the negative impacts of these cutbacks were captured in the following statement:

> I feel frustrated. My biggest frustration in this job is that someone is going to get hurt. And my fear is that I can't stop it. I'm afraid that something will happen. Something stupid. Someone will get shot or stabbed. And if I am doing my job, I've got to be able to see that. I have to be able to diffuse it before it happens. And without an extra vice-principal, without hall monitors, I'm running full time. I am a vice-principal. I should not be doing this. This is not my frigging job. I'm here at 9:00 at night doing a door check, because we have 64 outside doors in this building that get pennied by the gang guys to keep their guns in this building. So, it's 9:00 at night and I'm walking around thinking, "What the hell am I doing?"

Although Greg's middle-class location was not as acutely affected, district budget cutbacks also prevented him from meeting his own performance expectations and working proactively to support staff and students. The loss of the feelings of competence and self-efficacy which he had developed as an experienced teacher-leader led to feelings of "self-reproach" and frustration at "being set up by the system."

> So, there is a sense of feeling set up in this position. We are set up. Whether it's a software program that is new and it fails you and then you present X to the teachers and you know very well that it is full of mistakes. But that's the best you can do under the circumstances. But that's not good enough.

He expressed his anger at senior officials whom he felt only paid lip service to the assistant principals, but were not committed to improving their working conditions:

> I am tired of hearing principals and superintendents and directors and ministers saying that our job is so valued and so important. And I am tired of listening to that. I am. Don't tell me that you value me. Demonstrate that you value it. And if you can't, say, "I wish I could."

This combination of system inefficiencies, ongoing negative socialization impacts, and the loss of supportive networks contributed to the disintegration of the assistant principals' incoming commitment to make a difference for students and to improve schools. As Jerry reflected on his frustrations at his inability to create viable learning opportunities for students, he commented:

> So maybe, I'll get better at it, maybe I'll get better at not caring. You know, which is the other thing? You just don't care. And you start shutting down those kinds of processes that you have to block out. And you say, "I'm sorry, it just doesn't bother me." And I see it with other people. I see it with other vice-principals where they just kick the kid out. There is zero tolerance. There is no process. It's just boom. Get out!

While Jerry's comment communicated his anger at his school district's negligence, it also showed how the lack of district support can lead to growing intolerance toward students. A similar sense of disengagement from individual student concerns was echoed by other administrators. For Esther, who had dreamed of changing the system to create more equitable conditions for students, of letting go and distancing herself emotionally from her work was a painful turning point:

> Emotionally, I have said to myself, I cannot internalize everything and I have to take a broader look at students and the relationship between how I can achieve the best for them. I realize that I cannot save everybody and I get distressed over the fact that I have to ignore some of the ones who need it. It's difficult to let go.

Reintegration – Holding On and Reframing

While the process of Disintegration and digging deeper required letting go of and divesting themselves of some of their incoming dreams, expectations, and skills, the assistant principals described a complementary process of Reintegration. In contrast to the feelings of fragmentation and frustration which typified the Disintegration cycle, Reintegration involved holding on to, reframing, and adopting attitudes, skills, and behaviors which were more suitable to the demands of assistant principals' administrative roles. Part of this internal process included examining their existing bank of competencies, determining which of them would be useful in their new role, and reframing those chosen to meet the requirements of their new position. This reassessment allowed the assistant principals to recognize and accept their own, as well as their role's limitations, and it also generated an increased awareness of their strengths.

A corresponding aspect of the Reintegration entailed reinvesting themselves in their role and school environment by actively engaging in constructive roles and using their skills in meaningful ways. Although some of these attempts at reintegrating were initiated during the Emersion phase of the second epicycle, it was only after the assistant principals had experienced the full school year cycle that they were able to achieve a clearer perspective of their role and its social boundaries. The following comment by Greg highlights experience as an important variable in developing a clearer perspective of his role:

> I've done most things already twice, and so it wasn't just beginner's luck. And the things that I did wrong, I've done them differently. Not necessarily most correctly, but I've done them differently. So there is that evidence there that I am not falling in that same pothole every single time. So I think people have let go of that. And that's a wonderful feeling.

Reintegrating themselves into their role and environment also entailed reaching outward, and it involved a mutual give-and-take between the assistant principals and the social environment. This was evidenced in more purposeful attempts to impose their own values and skills on their role and to find spaces to exercise personal agency. In order to tolerate the provisional and variable nature of the role, and to counteract its negativity, the assistant principals sought out more positive people, roles, and activities. Although administrative socialization dynamics pressured them to let go of their classroom teaching relationships, they were able to retool their teaching skills to support students, staff, and parents. In spite of their loss of membership from the teaching corps, the assistant principals also reported initiating supportive relationships with vulnerable teachers, such as new recruits and more experienced faculty who were experiencing difficulties in their classrooms.

Michael connected this shift to the skills he had developed as a classroom teacher and curriculum leader. Having developed a clearer perspective of the tasks and boundaries of his role, he was able to find spaces where he could integrate his teaching skills into his administrative role and fulfill his goal to support his community:

> I have a role now and I understand my role and I have parameters I have to work within. But, like I am always teaching...Teaching staff to be better, teaching students to be better, teaching problem solving. Like, I am teaching all the time. It's not just in the classroom.

Similarly, Sandy, who had voiced concerns in the second cycle about expectations of her role as the "enforcer" described how she was able to reframe her role by finding "teachable moments" in which to work with students. While acknowledging the constraints imposed by district and ministry disciplinary policies and procedures, she underscored the importance of resisting these external configurations:

> The more you perceive your role as the police of the school, the more likely you are to be very stressed out. Or, that your role is to sort of "get those kids", rather than to just bring them in and work with them. Work through something with them, rather than to throw the book at them. It's just the philosophy. You have to do all of those things at some point, but you don't have to do them every day, and in every situation.

The assistant principals also intentionally sought out opportunities to work with clubs and teams, so that they could maintain contact with the positive students and teachers within the school. Greg stressed the importance of maintaining continued "vigilance" in this area, and he described the internal messages he used in order to resist and balance the negative aspects of his role:

> Get up off the chair and put yourself in situations where you are getting the entire gamut of the kids. Go to sit at the bench when you are watching a hockey game or a performance and right away the kids and everybody perceive you as a member of that community, not just as the one who is isolated in that office.

Some of the assistant principals also discovered that their cultural backgrounds were important assets in helping minority parents navigate the school system. For example, Andrew derived satisfaction from his work as a cultural interpreter and counselor to Chinese parents who felt intimidated by their lack of English:

> These parents are usually quite emotional when they do manage to sit down in the office and express themselves in Chinese...Finally, they could actually speak to someone about the cultural conflicts that they experienced in raising their children.

Assistant principals like Barb, Esther, Sandy, and Jerry who worked in economically disadvantaged schools were also involved in initiatives which were directed toward helping students academically and socially by addressing chronic problems, such as illiteracy and hunger. Barb was actively involved in raising funds for an on-site Breakfast Club which was designed to address problems of poverty within her school, and Sandy and Jerry were involved in in-school programs to support literacy initiatives. Although these projects were not as far-reaching as they anticipated during the earlier Entry–Exit and Immersion–Emersion epicycles, they cohered with the assistant principals' original motives to improve schools for students and staff, and they experienced pride in such accomplishments.

Andrew and Barb were also in the process of looking outside of their school for opportunities which would allow them to achieve a wider system impact. For example, Barb was working actively on a large-scale district effort on curriculum modifications for students with learning disabilities, and Andrew was also involved in a project to mentor new assistant principals. Participating in these activities allowed the assistant principals to counter the narrow institutional definitions of their role. The Disintegration–Reintegration epicycle provided the assistant principals with a different perspective on their pathway and their degree of fit with their school environment and administrative role. At this stage, they were able to construct more realistic maps of the administrative landscape and were in the process of carving out their own administrative route and territory. With this perspective, they were better equipped to understand the boundaries and aporias they had encountered in their previous trajectory and were ready to move on to the final cycle of Transformation–Restabilization which is discussed in Chapter 8.

Chapter 8
Transformation–Restabilization: Becoming and Being an Assistant Principal

Abstract Chapter 8 describes the final epicycle of Transformation–Restabilization. At this point in their transition, assistant principals are fully incorporated into the administrative and school culture and have developed the capacity to perform their role. Becoming and being an assistant principal is an interactive process of negotiation, construction, and maintenance which requires fundamental shifts in identity, values, perception, and behaviors. Key aspects of this process entail distancing from teaching and developing the cognitive, emotional, and social capacity to balance their ongoing leadership and management challenges.

The fourth epicycle of Transformation–Restabilization represents the culminating phase of the transition passage and it is a function of the cumulative experiences of the preceding cycles. This phase of the assistant principal's journey is consistent with transformation theories which identify structural changes that result in fundamental shifts in beliefs, values, perspectives, and frames of reference (Cranton, 2006; Mezirow, 2002). Transition and socialization theories also identify a period of adjusting to external demands and an ensuing stage of stability when transitioners are fully reincorporated into their new environment (Hart, 1993; Nicholson, 1990; Van Gennep, 1960). At this stage, new administrators feel socially and psychologically located within the organizational context, and they perform behaviors which are congruent with its norms and values (Ashforth & Saks, 1996). They also feel better equipped to deal with its challenges and to impose their own constructions on their role.

The assistant principals' administrative transformation was a process of being and becoming (Greenfield, 1985a; Matthews & Crow, 2003) which entailed a reorientation in goals, behaviors, and professional perspectives. It was evident in their disassociation from teaching and acceptance of the expectations and behaviors associated with the assistant principalship. A cooccuring cycle of Restabilization marked their return to a state of relative stability. While the first three epicycles were characterized by disequilibrium and dislocation, the assistant principals were able to achieve a sense of balance during the fourth epicycle. This was facilitated by feelings of emotional connection and belonging to their school community and the administrative reference group. Having developed competence in dealing with the conflicts and ambiguities of their role, the assistant principals also expressed confidence in their ability to anticipate its challenges and to balance their personal and organizational lives.

By the third year, the assistant principals had acquired a wide range of experiences which led to a more realistic understanding of their role and the development of relevant administrative skills and competencies. These included developing experience with the rhythm of the school year cycle, familiarity with the structures and cultures of their school district, and facility with educational politics, policies, and practices. This feeling of flow and stability was communicated by Barb as she compared her first and third years:

> It's like it's the third year now and it flows together. There's not a heck of a lot that is put on my plate that I can't figure out how to deal with it, I can't ask someone about, or get information from.

In order to make the transformation from teacher to administrator, the assistant principals had to find ways to resolve the social and psychological tensions they encountered at the different stages of their transitional trajectory. Part of this internal and external shift entailed constructing an administrative identity and developing the interpersonal and intrapersonal capacity and competence to negotiate the demands of their role.

Constructing an Administrative Identity

Studies of new front-line administrators show that climbing the hierarchical ladder of power and authority requires changes on the social, cognitive, and emotional levels (Armstrong, 2005, in press-a; Sigford 1998). As they acquire the skills and competencies to manage people and lead organizations, novice administrators undergo social and psychological shifts which facilitate adjustment to the demands of their role environment and the norms and expectations of their reference group (Freedman, 1998; Hill, 1992; Nicholson, 1990). These interpersonal and intrapersonal changes include developing new habits of mind, frames of reference, commitments, and behaviors which are more congruent with the expectations of their role and the collective beliefs of their surrounding ethos (Dotlich et al., 2004; Freedman, 1998). They also lead to the construction and evolution of new narratives, perspectives, and identities which reflect their emerging role constructions and professional contexts more accurately (Armstrong, 2005, in press-a).

The assistant principals' narratives suggest that being and becoming an administrator is an evolving spiral of perspective and identity transformation which is shaped by a complex interplay of individual and organizational forces. Meijers' (1998, 2002) description of identity construction as a co-constructed developmental learning process, or a "self narrative," bears some similarity to the assistant principals' experiences. He proposes that career identities emerge from reciprocal interactions between external organizational role demands and the psychological needs for making meaning. In order to develop a role identity and personal direction, individuals negotiate between themselves and others regarding the ways in which organizational roles and reality should be interpreted. These experiences are further assimilated into meaningful structures which consciously link personal motivations, interests, and competencies with chosen career roles. This is an iterative cognitive process which leads to a reconstructed self and perspective:

> To sum up, identity construction is seen to be a circular learning process, in which experiences and the self-concept are related through using concepts and endowing them with personal sense. In this process, identifications with persons, roles, organizations, values, and the like are constituted by reinterpretation of the self and the situation. Identity is a configuration of meanings, but this configuration will change constantly when new elements are given a place and are related to experiences. (Meijers, 2002, p. 160)

Transformation theorists also propose that changes emerge from reciprocal interactions between individuals and their external environments. Drawing on Piaget's work on assimilative and accommodative processes, Kegan (2000) highlights the cognitive nature of transformational changes. Focusing on the content and process of learning formation, he distinguishes between informative and transformative types of learning. Informative learning involves filling an existing form or schema and does not change its structure, while transformative learning puts it at risk, leading to structural change and increased capacity. He points out that transformation involves:

> Moving away from being "made up by" the value and expectations of the "surround"....
> that get uncritically internalized and with which one becomes identified, toward developing an internal authority that makes choices about these external values and expectations according to one's self-authored belief system. One goes from being psychologically "written by" the socializing press to "writing upon" it, a shift from a socialized to a self-authoring epistemology ... (p. 59)

As the assistant principals described the process of being and becoming an administrator, they drew on metaphors which communicated a paradoxical process of informing, conforming, and transforming that led to the development of their administrative identity. Both Andrew and Jerry invoked construction images to illustrate how they changed as a result of their administrative transition. Jerry's image of an unfinished project captured the formative nature of identity and perspective construction as it evolves within a difficult and changing working environment. As he reflected on his evolution as an administrator, he observed:

> I haven't come to a spot where I just am happy with how I am doing everything or how everything is going. I can put it this way. Like, I'm building a house, and I'm sweaty and tired and I still have lots of bricks to put on. And I can't get to that point when I'm standing on the roof and I am thinking, "This is a pretty good house." I haven't got there yet.

Describing his evolution as an assistant principal as a process of trial and error, Andrew used the metaphor of a workshop to illustrate this formative process. As he reflected on the changes he experienced as he progressed from his first to third year, he identified his ability to shift his focus from tasks to people as critical to constructing an administrative identity and perspective:

> I always think about it like a woodworking shop and for some reason we are given some tools to work with. In other words, we practice in our first year making some mistakes and

then grab another piece and do it again. It was absolutely task oriented. I made sure that I can handle this task or that task...The third year now, I'm not overly concerned about my ability to handle tasks, but it's more like walking around and relating to different people within that workshop and spending a little bit more time in the relationship piece with different players in that work room. That's the mental picture I have in terms of this transition. You tend to be very task oriented... Now, I'm more concerned with how people react, and also to foresee how people may react even before the situation occurs.

Barb's description of her evolution from teacher to administrator illustrated some of the dynamics which shaped her identity transformation. While her image of a sunflower in bloom suggested a positive transformation, her last sentence communicated the ongoing nature of the tension between internal and external forces:

I kind of think of being a flower in the bud while you are waiting to be called up to be a vice-principal and when you are waiting, you're like, "I just want to do it." Just call me. Give me a school. I'm ready. I'm ready. And then you get one and you explode all over the place... I am a sunflower with all the frigging crows pecking at my head all the time.

Like Barb, Greg made connections between environmental factors and the identity changes he experienced. As he reflected on the transformational changes that occurred as he moved from teacher to administrator, he pointed to personality and perspective changes which involved a progression from creativity, fluidity, and questioning to conservatism, inflexibility, and adherence to rules. He likened this to a pervasive reprogramming process which communicates normative pressures regarding how assistant principals should dress, speak, communicate, and behave.

You are being reprogrammed... So you are redefining yourself by the way you define those around you. I think it was Kant who said that you define yourself by the way you define those around you. And, now that you are hanging out with different people professionally, you have no choice but to see things differently.

The assistant principals connected their ability to "see things differently" to disassociating from their teaching identities and developing new ways of thinking, emoting, and behaving which were more aligned with an administrative perspective. Greg's notion of metamorphosis illustrated the depth and breadth of identity transformation and the paradoxes inherent within the process of being and becoming an assistant principal:

So there is this entire metamorphosis if you will, from free flowing to rigid. From organic to very structured and I think that that is the change that occurs in this particular position. You are more than who you are. That you are less than who you are is also true.

As he reflected on his earlier struggle to hold on to his teacher identity, Greg indicated that in spite of their resistance and reservations, novices who choose to remain in administrative roles eventually capitulate because of the external pressure to comply with institutional definitions of their role and their intrinsic need to connect with a social entity which was larger than themselves. Greg acknowledged that in spite of his attempts to resist to these pressures, over time, he came to accept these external definitions as an integral part of his administrative and role identity even when they conflicted with his preferences. He observed, "It was significant for me to make the realization and accept that this is the position I am in, rather than fighting it, because I haven't liked it very much."

The assistant principals' reflections provide insight into the conflicts and complexities that accompany identity change processes and the reasons why novices conform to external role definitions which are inconsistent with their values. Similarly, Nicholson and West's (1988) analysis of new managers' identity changes connect these "transmutations" (p. 186) to a psychological need for an identity which motivates individuals to commit to the socialization process and to buy into organizational roles. For the assistant principals, these social and psychological tensions began during the first two epicycles and surfaced most prominently during the Disintegration–Reintegration cycle. It resulted in a resocialization (Fein, 1990) process which motivated them to shed their teaching perspective and to establish social and psychological distance from their former teaching landscape.

Reflecting on this identity transformation, Sandy observed sadly: "I don't identify with staff. I get along well with the staff and I make an effort to be collegial, but it is a very different loyalty, or I guess, identity." This disassociation from teaching is consistent with O'Connor and Wolfe's (1991) finding that "movement to a higher phase involves a differentiation and often a repudiation of what the self had been in its previous subjectiveness" (p. 327). In order to create alignment between their objective and subjective realities, the assistant principals had to develop a new repertoire of skills. These included building the social, cognitive, and emotional capacity and competence to deal with the internal and external challenges of their transition and finding ways to reinterpret their role.

Developing Interpersonal and Intrapersonal Competence

Studies of new managers make strong connections between role and identity construction and the development of relevant interpersonal and intrapersonal skills (Freedman, 1998; Hill, 1992). During the early stages of their transition, the assistant principals reported feelings of incompetence because their pre-role teaching experiences and principal certification courses did not provide them with the training or content knowledge required to perform their administrative role effectively. As they reflected on their transformation into administrators, the assistant principals linked their development of cognitive, emotional, and social competence to their ability to understand the possibilities and limitations of their role, their school environment, and themselves, while working under conditions of ambiguity and crisis. This required new ways of being, feeling, thinking, perceiving, and identifying which were more consistent with their administrative perspective. This meant accepting that they were no longer teachers and recognizing that stress, problem solving, and crisis management were endemic to their administrative role.

In-depth knowledge of their social, political, and cultural landscape was also seen by the assistant principals as critical to their competence as administrators. This involved gathering current and historical institutional information that would allow them to create accurate maps of and building a network of relationships with key stakeholders both inside and outside of their school. According to Greg, this required content and process knowledge related to the who, how, what, when, where, and why of administration, as well as the ability to recognize their own strengths and weaknesses, the boundaries and possibilities of their role, and their spheres of influence. Equally important was their awareness of their information gaps and their ability to demonstrate competence and confidence, in spite of the limitations and ambiguities of their role. Grey reflected:

> It may be semantics whether it's confident or comfortable, more knowledgeable, or more aware of what you know and don't know. That's the other part too. I am more aware of what I don't know. And being prepared to do well what I take on, but not to necessarily worry about the other areas that I don't take on.

Although they had anticipated working with children, the assistant principals were unprepared to deal with the relational aspects of management and the socioemotional stresses and strains that characterize middle management roles. They identified a lack of "hard and soft skills" as a key impediment to their ability to develop administrative competence. In order to address these deficits, they had to adopt a new set of dispositions, skills, and behaviors which would allow them to effectively manage and motivate a complex variety of individuals and groups, both inside and outside of their schools.

Building Networks and Relationships

The assistant principals reported that while technical skills were easier to acquire, developing personal and people management skills was more difficult because of the unpredictability of their role and the different people and constituency groups to whom they were accountable. Working with children and adults and creating sustainable relationships at the vertical and horizontal levels of the organizational hierarchy (i.e., supervisors, supervisees, assistant principal colleagues, and community members) was a challenging task. Negotiating this vast network of relationships required new levels of interpersonal and intrapersonal literacy which included communication, conflict, and crisis management skills, as well as the ability to read people and contexts, to shift their focus between tasks and processes, and to predict responses.

The assistant principals identified learning to work with, through, and around individuals and groups as critical to their ability to navigate the social landscape. Building relationships was integral to this process, and it entailed continuously seeking out and developing reliable networks and alliances which would facilitate their ability to manage schools proactively and to impose a leadership framework on their role. These relationships were developed through formal and informal interactions, and the assistant principals used terms such as "schmoozing," "positioning," "doing favors," "calling in favors," "smoothing the waters," and "sucking up" to describe the broad range of interpersonal tactics they used to motivate others. While personality and context factors were deemed important, the assistant principals identified experience and time as critical to their ability to negotiate the idiosyncratic characteristics of their communities. As Barb compared the early stages of her transition to her current position, she highlighted time and experience as key to building credibility, trust, and respect:

> It takes time to build trust and that has implications for your work. After you have been an administrator, you have a collection of people that you can call and get assistance from, whereas, when I was a beginning vice-principal, I didn't have that. And, I think again, it goes back to that relationship building as being so incredibly important. If you are not a people person it's a problem. So I think relationship building is number one, and being able to see it before it sees you is number two. So being proactive is important.

Greg also connected time and interpersonal competence to gaining knowledge of the strengths and dispositions of his constituents. He also pointed out that, in many ways, the skills required to be a successful administrator were an extension of the relationship building skills that he had developed in the classroom:

> I really believe that good teaching practices translate well into administrative and educational leadership practices. If students and staff feel that there is a safety net of respect and dignity they will be willing to take a chance. . .The other thing too, is that I know now whom I can call on in terms of staff and in terms of students. There are people I can call on for certain things. So that's starting to be established as your reputation, as well as the give-and-take that goes back and forth, and who's amiable in certain situations and who's not. I think that's the real strength of a principal or vice-principal who has been in the position for a long time. Just to know where you can go.

Cultivating a network of reliable workers and supporters and demonstrating trust were described as critical to constructing interpersonal relationships. As he described the process of building alliances within and across groups and elaborated on the importance of time, Greg compared relationship building to breaking down the various walls and barriers that existed in the school culture. He emphasized the need for assistant principals to demonstrate sensitivity to between-group boundaries and to work hard to build trust and respect:

> With a novice administrator time is a factor and human beings take a long time to trust and it may take a year or two. So, the time factor works against any new administrator because you are also moving into their school and there will be tension about administrators moving through *my* space. So, you really have to work hard as a new administrator to earn and to demonstrate that this is your community. But, you have to remember that it was theirs first. You are moving into somebody else's home, some may have been there for 25 years and some for 30 years. They have a history and a culture and they are cynical about the conveyor belt of administrators moving through their space. So, that's one of the first things you have to be aware of and you have to see yourself as earning the right, but not in terms of your title, but in terms of your responsibilities and obligations. I am talking about the soft culture of earning a right and demonstrating that in fact this place is yours from the get go. So, you stop referencing back to your previous school. You stop using the language of "When I worked at X school I did this and that". They don't want to know about that even though it informs what you do. They think, "This is my school, you are coming into my territory as an administrator". So teachers and parents see you as an intruder, and that is one of the walls and one of the boxes you have to break down. And, you do it through hard work, dignity, serving, and being responsible.

Barb also identified establishing strong alliances at the school and district levels as a critical foundation for leadership and change. This entailed being active and proactive, demonstrating credibility by working "above and beyond the call of duty," following through on commitments to staff and students, motivating others, and liaising with community members on an ongoing basis. She observed,

> I think the biggest thing about being a vice-principal is building relationships as well. So, I think a lot of things are probably prevented by having good relationships with people in the building, and there will always be people who you won't click with. But I think by being available and being a hard worker and being a participant in the school, *that* helps build relationships with teaching staff and kids and therefore I think that's what keeps people active as well.

While Sandy also agreed that good relationships and hard work were key aspects of developing competence, she reiterated the need for assistant principals to reflect on the quality and purpose of those relationships. This meant intentionally creating relationships which would bring about positive changes for students and actively getting out in the school community to include a representative spectrum of individuals from different backgrounds:

> I think leadership for me especially in an inner city school is about working with people to influence them to accomplish something good. So, I think a great deal of time and effort needs to be spent cultivating relationships. Making people feel comfortable....And, you do that by being visible around the building, interacting with people more often, recognizing them for what they do, and also involving them in processes of opinion within the school. And, I always try to avoid setting up a system where there is a pecking order or the perception thereof, where it's only a few people who are constantly being called on. So if I have something, I will go out – physically go out – and try to recruit people. And I look at diversity. That's very important to me.

However, although the assistant principals discussed the importance of working closely with all members of their community, their conversations focused primarily on the challenge of working with teaching faculty in non-adversarial ways. For the most part, the assistant principals engaged in instrumental relationships with faculty which were related to attempts to get faculty to "buy in" to school and district goals. These interactions were focused primarily on school initiatives, professional development, and support. They alternated between supervision, discipline, collaboration, and personal support, and they included activities such as committee work, mentoring, coaching, and instructional support. While these relationships were collegial on the surface, they often involved a complex political dance of moves and counter moves because of the assistant principals' lack of institutional power, their reliance on teachers to implement policies, and their fear of union repercussions.

Developing relationships of trust was seen as indispensable in bringing teachers on board, and it entailed involving teachers in formal and informal decision-making processes. In many instances, the assistant principals admitted that although they believed that they could find more efficient solutions to a number of problems, they initiated consultative and interactive problem-solving processes, so that teachers would commit to district and school-based initiatives. Andrew described collaborative decision making as important in building collegiality and creating a sense of community and ownership for outcomes. He advised, "You may already have the solution, but you have to go through the consultation part and make other people feel that they are involved and that it's our solution it's not only your solution."

Leading by example was also identified as important in building trust and establishing credibility with teaching faculty. This required the assistant principals to demonstrate competence and commitment to hard work, and it entailed working long hours, fulfilling disciplinary roles, and performing supervisory tasks, such as covering classes and doing hallway and cafeteria duties which teaching faculty were reluctant to do. Barb acknowledged the symbiotic nature of these administrative/teacher relationships and the importance of using a variety of approaches in order to motivate teachers to support school and district goals:

> People will get down in the dirt and do the work because they see you get down in the dirt and work. Because they are the ones that are going to be on the front line getting their hands dirty. And, it's not just a matter of here is a policy they need to do it. It's the whole coaxing, it's the relationship, it's the training, it's making them buy into it and making them feel that it is important, making them want to do it. That's leadership. It's the people piece.

While these efforts were directed toward improving schools, they were often transactional in nature. Reflecting on the importance of good relationships to their work, the assistant principals pointed out that investing in these relationships was beneficial during periods of labor unrest. For example, having established relationships of trust and mutual dependence, the assistant principals and their faculty engaged in acts of creative insubordination during teacher strikes or when they were pressured by their school districts and unions to implement policies and directives that worked against student achievement. However, implicit in this social contract was the commitment to buffer and protect teachers from students, parents, and other community members. While these transactional relationships sometimes paid off during periods of heightened tension and uncertainty, these tacit arrangements sometimes tempered the assistant principals' ability to address inappropriate teacher behaviors.

The assistant principals also identified power imbalances and a fear of teacher conflict and union grievances as ongoing challenges which impeded them from exercising their authority in an ethical manner. A common source of tension related to students who were unjustly treated by teachers. Although the assistant principals often agreed with students when they were sent to the office without due cause, they were reluctant to challenge or discipline teachers because of the potential backlash. As Esther reflected on the challenge of dealing with negative teacher behaviors and the potential political repercussions, she observed,

> Because you could come on harsh, just lay it down and just state, "You do not do this anymore". But you have to create an amicable situation and work with them in a professional way. So, *that* I find is very difficult because I don't want to offend in the sense that I may create difficulty for myself later by doing that. But, I don't hesitate to tell them what's correct and what's right. But at the same time that can be a setback.

Greg also identified articulating a commitment to students and having ongoing conversations with teachers about common goals, values, and responsibilities as key to resolving conflicts with teachers and building a common vision:

> The similarities have to be reinforced all the time, that is, the common focus of why we are all here together in this place. And, the common focus obviously is the child. So you continuously have to remind teachers that your goal is not to make their job difficult. Your goal is the same as theirs. You also have to continuously have the conversation of what is common. "What do we all have in common?" One of the ways to do it in terms of a school is to insinuate that there are students in every community. And by doing that, then in fact it is about the child, and it's also about them. Then, there are the conversations, whether it is timetabling, whether it's the courses they're going to be teaching, whether it's the exam schedule, anything like that. It has to be framed in terms of, "This is not punitive, to ensure that you work from 9–5." But rather "If we both have the child's best interest in common, then how do we collectively address that?", rather than setting ourselves up as oppositional to one another.

Sandy also underscored the need for assistant principals to assert their authority wisely in order to avoid conflicts. This entailed being "authoritative without being authoritarian," and demonstrating "wisdom about the so-called powers of this job." She observed:

> I think one has to carry a certain confidence in the role and a certain level of independent thinking, because if you are forever being led or being dictated to you by anyone, then you wonder who is in charge. And, when I say that, it's not about that power again. You do have to have a certain level of authority. That comes with it. It is an expectation.

These ongoing dynamics reflect the development of the assistant principals' administrative identity and their ability to build viable external networks and alliances. They were also integral to their ability to develop the inner capacity to manage the cognitive and emotional strains of their role and to successfully navigate the administrative passage.

Developing Cognitive and Emotional Competence

Becoming an administrator exposed the assistant principals to an unaccustomed range of management and leadership dilemmas which pushed their psychological boundaries and destabilized their professional identities. The ongoing tensions of dealing with a conflicting range of issues, and being constantly on guard for crises, led to superficial and fragmented emotions, thoughts, behaviors, and solutions and feelings of incompetence. The assistant principals' stability and maintenance roles required them to deal with a wide variety of people and problems and to exert control in the presence of serious crises. Michael's comment captures the burden of this responsibility and the cognitive and emotional challenge of dealing quickly and effectively with such crises on a daily basis:

> I guess I am responsible. It comes down to responsibility for the fallout that happens from a decision that I make or the team makes. I have to respond to the parent who complains. I have to respond to the teacher. If students are going crazy in the class, people are going

to look to me for some kind of response. And so I try to make sure that I have as much information as I can to make the best decision.

In order to manage the cognitive and emotional aporias of their role, the assistant principals had to develop new approaches and competencies which would allow them to work proactively with their communities to improve their schools. This involved building the mental capacity to deal with the fragmentation of thought, action, and emotion that characterized their middle-space roles and devising frameworks and schemas to resolve problems. The assistant principals identified problem solving and exercising good judgment and wisdom as critical to developing cognitive competence. Andrew observed,

> Because so much in our job really depends on our judgment. And, our judgment comes from the confidence and our experience. So there should be some kind of a training process that would help them to ease into this job.

The assistant principals described exercising judgment as making decisions from an aggregate perspective, considering people, processes, procedures and outcomes, as well as short-term impacts. This required developing the skills and capacity to manage data, to conceptualize, resolve, and anticipate a wide variety of problems, and to minimize fallout. Key aspects of this administrative skill-set entailed gathering and processing information from diverse sources, asking questions, reading between the lines, weighing multiple needs and outcomes, making quick decisions with incomplete and often contradictory reports, and doing damage control. The assistant principals reported that, over time, this approach to problem solving became part of their mind-set. As Karen illustrated how problem solving from an aggregate perspective pervaded her way of thinking and being, she reported that her friends often commented on how she now thought and behaved like an administrator, even when she was outside of school:

> When they point out something, I look at the overall situation and say, well, it could be this or this might have happened. That's part of the job. When you are trying to solve a situation, you want to look at it from various angles. You talk to the teacher, the student, other administrators, etc. I think my friend described it as looking at the bigger issue rather than the immediate little problem. I am learning not to react. There are times when I think I have to do this right away, but then I can sit back and look at the situation.

The assistant principals identified the ability to handle and communicate emotions appropriately as an important part of demonstrating administrative competence and building relationships of trust. Schein (1978) identifies emotional competence as at the core of the transformation process, and he indicates that "the essence of the general manager's job is to absorb the emotional strains of uncertainty, interpersonal conflict, and responsibility" (p. 167). In order to develop emotional competence, the assistant principals had to build the emotional capacity to deal with the ongoing shocks, surprises, and absurd contrasts of their role and to inure themselves against the unpredictability and stress of their role. As part of this process, the assistant principals had to accept the fragmented nature of their role and the fact that their days would be unpredictable. Sandy emphasized the importance of having a general plan, developing a flexible attitude, prioritizing tasks, and letting go of the sense of mastery and control that, as teachers, they had come to expect in their classrooms:

> The key to not becoming too stressed is to recognize that the day is full of surprises and that you can't have a rigid plan. . .You devote all your energies to the problem, and you move on to what could have waited. You can't get worked up about it.

Since exhibiting emotions in public was considered a sign of weakness, part of demonstrating emotional competence entailed projecting an image of calm, confidence, and efficiency and masking their emotions. The assistant principals used terms such as "posturing," "faking it," "pretending a level of confidence," and "not letting them smell fear" to describe how they communicated emotional competence and a sense of control in the face of conflict and crisis. These attempts at impression management are consistent with previous studies of new administrators which identify an organizational ethos that negates the role of emotion in educational administration. For example, Marshall's (1985a) research on the enculturation of assistant principals indicates that "covering" or finding ways to cope with that shock and continuing to appear competent, calm, and loyal are essential enculturation tasks (p. 43). Sigford's (1998) research on new administrators also found that they were expected to be emotionally detached from information and that confidence in them decreased when they were perceived as too demonstrative. She observed that:

> Women learn to close their door and emote in private, maintaining a public persona of control. For women and persons of different cultures who have been allowed to express feelings, it is difficult to come to a middle ground of expressing feelings from a detached perspective. (p. 33)

The following observations by Greg illustrate how external role expectations of detachment influence assistant projections of emotional competence and become embodied over time at the physical and psychological levels:

> You don't share all of your anxiety and angst with your staff. That's not your role. They are also not in a position to have intimate conversations with you everyday. So it is a very isolating. . . So physically, it drains us. The other aspect of physically, is if you are upset or happy, when a teacher asks you how you are, they don't want to know that you are upset or happy. They don't want to know. It's a courtesy so when you are out here, put on the myriad of faces that are accessible to you and be appropriate and polite, even when you don't feel like it.

In order to manage their emotional boundaries and to buffer themselves from the emotional impact of their role, the assistant principals learned to distance themselves psychologically from the negative fallout of their role and to deflect criticism over time. They described this stance as "developing a thick skin," "knowing my bottom line," and "not taking it personally." As Sandy reflected on an emotionally draining relationship with a parent who had launched a complaint against her, she stressed the importance of having internal and external feedback mechanisms in place in order to help process these difficult events:

> You do tend to take things less personally and you develop a thick skin. If the incident with the mother had happened in February a year ago, I would have considered leaving, or be so paranoid thinking, "Is that a reflection of my incompetence?" But I am more confident that

I have a process and I work through things and I reflect back on what I do. Yes, I did the right thing and that reaction is a normal reaction for that person... And you have to learn to not take it personally. They only look at you for what you represent, so there is nothing personal about it.

The strategies of distancing and developing increased "toughness" helped the assistant principals to rationalize some of the anger that was directed at their role and to reduce the dissonance between their ideal and actual roles. However, as Barb indicated, it was not always possible to deflect these negative onslaughts and she questioned the cumulative impact on her psyche:

And again, there's the whole thing about how to not take what's coming at you as personally... about how it's somebody else [who is] just venting and you become the venting board. But how much do you really need to take of that?

Developing the emotional capacity to resolve these internal and external challenges helped temper the pain of handling chronic difficulties. However, the assistant principals were not always comfortable with their responses because they often reinforced the status quo.

Finding Meaning and Restoring Balance

Transition and transformation studies establish strong connections between identity construction and intrapersonal competence, and they propose that individuals seek to balance their social and emotional worlds as they integrate changes into their personal and professional lives (Abrego & Brammer, 1992; Hill, 1992). Meijers (2002) describes identity formation as "a process in which cognitions and emotions are balanced gradually and in a dialogical way" (p. 158). He also indicates that this balance facilitates sense making, which leads to reconfigured narratives and motivated action:

Meaning can thus be defined as cognition brought in balance with will and emotion. Balancing cognition, will and emotion is a process that never ends because individuals continuously undergo new experiences that force them to redefine the meaning of old ones (i.e., to rewrite parts of their biography), which often results in new motivations to act. (Meijers, 1998, p. 201).

While their socializing challenges had not changed significantly, the assistant principals were better able to assert themselves because of the strength of their networks and relationships. However, their ability to exercise this level of role management and maintenance was only achieved with time, administrative experience, and a deeper understanding of school and school district structures and policies.

The assistant principals identified "developing perspective" as essential to cognitive and emotional growth and balance, and they connected this to the learning derived from their successes and failures and a deeper understanding of the boundaries and pitfalls of the educational landscape. Developing a better understanding of their role relative to other institutional actors was also important to perspective development. The assistant principals pointed out that their ability to develop a balanced perspective and to influence the "bigger picture" was dependent on their principal's leadership style and the amount of power he or she was willing to share with them. As Sandy reflected on the need for assistant principals to exercise authority and judgment, she highlighted the importance of knowing the limitations and possibilities of her role:

> But, always in the back of my mind it is about that whole idea of perspective, representation, meaning, needing to know that I can contribute something by being involved. I think as a vice-principal, you are not going to pull the same amount of clout as the principal. And I think that's the difference. But it's not necessarily about the clout. There is that kind of pecking order that is very alive between the principal and vice-principal. We are not even a role in the education act. Apparently, it's kind of a made up position. So you're kind of like the sidekick a lot of the time, in some places more so than others. Again depending on leadership styles, a vice-principal might, because of the generosity of the principal, be infused with more authority and involvement. And in other places it's very much a control dominated relationship.

All of the assistant principals expressed a commitment to supporting students and staff, and they identified sustaining healthy relationships as a critical factor in their ability to impose a leadership framework on their role. Increased familiarity with their role and their context facilitated their ability to achieve their incoming goal of making a difference for students and staff, and they were able to mitigate the impact of their decisions on staff and students by "finding the gray areas" in policies and "bending the rules." Although these achievements were not as significant as they had initially conceived in the early Entry–Exit epicycle, they represented a source of personal satisfaction to the assistant principals and allowed them to resist negative images of themselves as punitive disciplinarians.

An integral part of this vision encompassed focusing on teacher mentoring and development as a means of improving students' academic outcomes and ensuring success. This commitment is captured in Jerry's comment:

> As you get older, you think that you should be mentoring and have more to offer, not just to people in your departments or your co-workers, but to others within you staff. So you have a vision of what you think you can do to make the educational system better and to make where you are working a better place.

To some extent, mentoring and supporting staff represented a form of resistance to socialization influences, where the assistant principals were able to communicate their own vision and values to teachers and other members of their community. This was done through instituting coaching and mentoring programs for new teachers and providing them with emotional and/or pedagogical support. The assistant principals were also actively involved in providing instructional and emotional support to teachers who were having difficulty, through direct interventions in the classroom, personal counseling, and instructional support. Coaching experienced teachers who were interested in developing their leadership skills or in assuming administrative positions was also identified as an important part of this process. Providing teachers with resources and facilitating opportunities for professional development aligned to their schools' goals and missions were also common interventions.

Thus, having developed more confidence in their abilities, the assistant principals were now able to balance some of the tensions of the role by openly articulating their own personal values. Reflecting on the conflicts that he had experienced with some of the veteran faculty, Andrew asserted:

> If I believe that something is not right I will stand up for my own position. Whether you are a classroom teacher or a department head, that doesn't matter. It doesn't mean that we cannot be diplomatic, but when it comes to principles and values, I believe that's important.

Sandy also highlighted the importance of bringing her own personal values into her enactment of the role as opposed to rigidly adhering to an external standard: "Regarding the transition, I am carrying out the duties of my position by imposing more of my own values on a lot of the decisions I make." Having intentionally chosen a more proactive approach to her role, she identified exercising wisdom, courage, and compassion, giving students "chances" and "taking risks" as important. This approach to her work was an ongoing moral and political struggle which required integrity, reflection, and a clear communication of values:

> I think a lot of it has to do with character. You do have to have a lot of clarity about who you are, and why you're doing something the way you're doing it. I think you also have to be willing to engage in a lot of inner dialogue about issues, do a lot of reflection, and ask a lot of questions about things. And not jump to conclusions very quickly, or feel that you must make decisions very quickly. You're there to make certain decisions about different perspectives and different levels of information. And, above anyone else, you have to be able to make the fairest or most equitable decision based on all of the information. So, being courageous enough to explain them and I think not to be intimidated. It is really about that value, inner core that you have, or philosophy and also how you project your confidence and your authority – not your power.

The assistant principals also stressed the need to balance the personal and professional spheres of their lives. As she reflected on the demanding nature of her role, Sandy identified establishing priorities and using her time wisely as important skills. She also emphasized the importance of separating her role identity from her personal identity as a spouse, parent, etc., outside of school:

> I try to balance time, really because as I said, there is a lot more to my identity and I really consider that more important than my role as a vice-principal. I have a private life and I really stick to that and maintain it and I try to separate the two. . .So you have to create a healthy balance between the professional and the personal. And recognize your humanity and your limitations. Your workday really should have a start and it should have an end. And when you are on site, use the time as efficiently as you possibly can.

Having resolved some of the contradictions of his administrative role, Greg reported having a more balanced personal and professional life. This was a provisional and precarious form of equilibrium which entailed balancing the absurd contrasts by maintaining perspective on a personal and professional level:

> So there is a balance in my life, and that is a peaceful state of being, which is very important. . . . Perspective is the challenge. Never, never lose perspective, and find people around you, whether it is your children or friends to bring perspective where you have none. And I also have been able to separate my job from my personal life. And be humble

and proud simultaneously. That is the perspective of absurd contrasts. Balance the absurd contrasts all the time and teeter totter on them. That's OK, just don't fall completely off.

He also underscored the importance of persistence and keeping students at the center of administrative practice.

> Keep that in balance, because I really believe that this is a continuation of what you are doing in the classroom. You have to be really stubborn. And I am not giving up my soul. And the soul of it is good education and great kids.

Levin (1999) describes transitions as a continuous negotiation of identities and meanings. Although the assistant principals were able to achieve a certain measure of equilibrium and stability as a result of their experiences, Restabilization was not a period of stasis. Adapting to ongoing reforms, new policies, and directives continued to be a challenge. The assistant principals' feelings of frustration were captured by Karen, who observed:

> I would say that it would be nice if I could effect change. Nowadays it has been a little difficult. Most of it has been reacting to situations. The timelines are very short and it's almost like you are reacting all the time.

Even though he felt comfortable in many areas of his role, Andrew also suggested that becoming an effective administrator entailed being in a constant state of adjustment because of the unpredictable nature of their role and changing school demographics. He observed:

> I always think back, when you mention about my transition, I believe that I am still in transition... But, my strongest experience in this process of the transition would be my very first year.

The assistant principals' experiences are consistent with Hart's (1993) observation that administrators must be constantly redefining themselves because of change factors which are inherent in the administrative role due to complex environments and rapid technological advances. She observes:

> When viewed cyclically, it requires that people continually project into the future, combining their appraisal and assessment of current work performance with preparation for future transitions into new leadership assignments. (p. 460)

With the exception of Jerry who had received clear signals from his supervisors that he would not be promoted, none of the assistant principals saw this position as a terminal stage of their administrative journey. They were either in the process of scanning the horizon for future possibilities or had already received confirmation that their names had been added to the district promotion list for the principalship, thus indicating the possibility of a new transformational trajectory.

Part III
The Way Forward: Connecting Theory and Practice

Do the difficult things while they are easy and do the great things while they are small. A journey of a thousand miles must begin with a single step.

Lao Tzu

Part III discusses the importance of the assistant principalship as an organizational leadership role. It raises critical questions regarding assistant principals' roles, and it calls for coordinated efforts by practitioners, theorists, and researchers to review current conceptions of this role. It proposes that theoreticians and practitioners need to work together to develop a clear articulation of the assistant principalship and to examine its importance in creating student success and effective schools. A deeper understanding of the personal, professional, and organizational aspects of administrative passages and transitions is also recommended. Building on suggestions made by assistant principals and the existing literature, this section also provides recommendations for improving the assistant principals' role, and for creating coordinated and sustainable structures that scaffold the developmental leadership needs of newcomers and support the creation of equitable communities of practice.

Chapter 9
Reconceptualizing Assistant Principals' Leadership Transitions

Abstract Chapter 9 focuses on the importance of reconceptualizing the assistant principalship and leadership transitions at the theoretical and practical levels. It proposes that understanding the personal, professional, and organizational aspects of administrative passages and transitions can address some of the existing leadership gaps and improve recruitment, selection, induction, and retention practices for this critical leadership position. This chapter provides recommendations for improving the assistant principals' role and for creating coordinated and sustainable structures that scaffold the leadership development needs of newcomers and support the creation of equitable communities of practice.

New assistant principals' narratives confirm that even though administrative passages are often embedded within the normal practices of schooling, they destabilize new administrators' inner psyches and influence their beliefs and actions in myriad ways. However, the actual and potential impact of this transition continues to be undervalued in academic research and in the everyday practices of schooling. These leadership passages carry important ramifications for the study and practice of school leadership and management. Assistant principals represent a critical mass of middle managers and, in many cases, the future face of upper-level management. As on-the-ground educational leaders, assistant principals play a critical role in implementing operational directives and reform policies, shaping school culture and influencing students' outcomes.

Theoretical and field-based configurations of administrative roles and leadership work conjointly to shape the direction and outcomes of policy, research, and training. These frameworks and metanarratives further determine the levels and types of respect and support that assistant principals receive. They also unintentionally contribute to a new administrator's success or failure. The potential negative fallout of uninformed decisions and actions on children's lives provides compelling reasons for research, training, and regulatory bodies to institute thoughtful, sustainable, and systematic approaches that can transform administrative practices in positive ways. The following sections provide recommendations for the ways in which some of these issues can be addressed.

D.E. Armstrong, *Administrative Passages*, Studies in Educational Leadership 4, DOI 10.1007/978-1-4020-5269-9_9, © Springer Science+Business Media B.V. 2009

Reconceptualizing Transitions and Passages: Theoretical Challenges

In spite of the fact that the assistant principalship has been an important leadership role for decades, it continues to be marginalized to a great degree within the theory and research of educational administration (Armstrong, 2005; Marshall & Hooley, 2006). This situation is directly linked to overarching metanarratives which assume that:

- School leadership only occurs at the top of the organizational hierarchy;
- Leadership is disassociated from management;
- Individuals' lived experiences can be adequately understood through an organizational lens;
- The assistant principalship is primarily a transitional role.

Expanding theoretical paradigms to include the assistant principalship as a de facto leadership role, listening to assistant principals' stories, and addressing issues which are directly related to their transitional experiences can illuminate these blind spots.

Researching Middle-Space Leadership

An accurate understanding of the complexity of educational leadership and assistant principals' transitions cannot be achieved without considering the standpoint of middle-level institutional leaders and the complex supporting roles they play (Armstrong, in press-a; Hartzell et al., 1994). While principals and assistant principals engage in important leadership roles and their functions and duties sometimes overlap, their experiences are not the same. Principals' and assistant principals' transitional and socialization impacts vary because of differences in their hierarchical locations and perspectives, their access to positional power and influence, as well as institutional constructions of their role (Armstrong, in press-a). Furthermore, assistant principals also have the added challenge of dealing with their principals' demands. Research studies that explore the following questions can provide a more detailed understanding of these issues:

- What leadership and management challenges do assistant principals experience as middle-level leaders?
- How do they negotiate leadership tensions and "absurd contrasts"?
- How are principals' and assistant principals' administrative passages alike or different?
- What are the challenges and dynamics of the administrative team?
- How can leadership teams and shared decision practices be most effectively coordinated and utilized?

Studying Individual Change and Transition

Studies of new managers show that although managerial career changes are often treated as discrete, linear events, they are actually experienced as continuous, unpredictable processes (Armstrong, 2004b; Dotlich et al., 2004; Hill, 1992; Leucke, 2003; Sigford, 1998). Although the dominant socialization paradigm provides a valuable lens on organizational practices, it does not capture the complexity of the personal change process and its impact on that individual. Furthermore, concentrating solely on external impacts portrays organizations as monolithic and individuals as passive and undifferentiated (Ashforth, 2001; Bullogh et al., 1991). This unintentionally downplays newcomer agency and the cognitive, emotional, and spiritual nature of transitions (Armstrong, 2005).

Research and theory which provides insight into assistant principals' leadership passages and their role in school reforms is urgently needed. In order for educational researchers to understand how educational practice is (re)produced, they must examine individuals' internal experiences (Kincheloe, 2003). Theoretical paradigms which conceptualize career passages and transitions as works in progress that begin during teaching and continue throughout the administrative career cycle can provide a deeper understanding of individual and group trajectories. Person-centered perspectives such as epicycles which evolve out of new assistant principals' narratives can be used by educational researchers to model internal change trajectories and bridge individual and organizational frames.

In addition to making broad generalizations about transitional experiences, researchers must also attend to the ways in which co-occurring locations of difference affect organizational passages. Feminist and antiracist scholars point to unequal class, gender, and ethnicity relations within educational administration and the tendency to privilege the experiences of white, able bodied, middle class, heterosexual males (Banks, 2000; Blackmore, 2002; Rusch, 2004). The assistant principals' stories and anecdotal evidence from practicing administrators also show that while school districts often espouse equity in theory, women and people of color are often discriminated against in practice.

Female and racial minority school administrators experience additional challenges because they often lack mentoring and support networks (Marshall & Hooley, 2006; Sigford, 1998). Transitional stress and burnout rates are also compounded for brown and black administrators like Jerry, Esther, and Sandy who are placed in high needs urban schools without training and resources. Quantitative and qualitative data regarding how minority group members navigate these challenges and how organizations engage in equitable and/or inequitable practices is needed. Some of the key questions which need to be explored are:

- What are the hiring and retention statistics for assistant principals?
- What are the statistics for minority group members, e.g., race, class, religion, ethnicity, disability, gender, sexual orientation?
- How do discriminatory organizational structures and processes impact assistant principals' attitudes and practices?

- What practices are perceived or experienced as discriminatory?
- How do assistant principals from different backgrounds navigate hiring and pro-motion barriers?
- How do they access mentoring, sponsorship, and coaching opportunities?
- Which organizational practices and structures ensure inclusion?

Research and theory which integrates and balances personal and organizational perspectives can provide a more comprehensive picture of the factors which support individual and organizational change and transformation. Accurate statistical infor-mation regarding the number of assistant principals and the different configurations of this role is also inadequate. Cross-national, international, and cross-cultural lon-gitudinal qualitative and quantitative studies that follow potential candidates during the pre- and post-promotion process can address this gap.

When used in conjunction with narrative approaches and located within theories of adult development, such studies may illustrate the psychological and social nature of perspective and identity construction and personal transformation. Important questions for theory and research which can improve the knowledge base include:

- How do assistant principals' narratives conflict and cohere with dominant orga-nizational theories and discourses?
- How do personal and organizational factors mediate assistant principal transi-tions?
- How do these factors impact assistant principals' emotions, attitudes, and perfor-mance?
- What personal and organizational factors promote assistant principal resilience, self-efficacy, and (dis)engagement?
- How do career-plateaued assistant principals negotiate their role?
- How can adult development theories enhance the knowledge base of educational administration?

By integrating knowledge and research about the various types of career transitions and by studying the micro and macro processes which administrators experiencing career transitions undergo, theoreticians can deepen understandings of administra-tive change phenomena and more accurately inform policy and practice.

Supporting Assistant Principals' Transitions: Practical Challenges

New assistant principals' narratives confirm previous studies asserting that although transitions influence behavior and success, newcomers and their organizations are generally unaware of such phenomena or how to deal with them (Ashforth, 2001; Bridges, 2001). In most cases, organizations behave as if their responsibility begins and ends with recruitment, and there are few coordinated attempts to facilitate the joining-up process (Nicholson & West, 1989). New administrators are often overwhelmed by the magnitude of this change process and they feel abandoned by their organizations (Armstrong, 2005; Sigford, 1998).

Within the field of education, administrative transitions are often missed opportunities for new assistant principals' leadership development, community growth, and educational change. Factors such as inappropriate training, haphazard induction and placement processes, poor communication, and inappropriate feedback contribute to new administrators' transitional strain. Although shocks and surprises are intrinsic to transitions and passages, a number of the technical, psychosocial, and physical hurdles that new assistant principals experience can be averted by appropriate and conscious preparation, planning, and support at the institutional and individual levels.

Malone (2001) observes that while almost everyone agrees that administrators need formal training to prepare for their positions, few agree on what the nature of the training should be. In order to ensure effective, inclusive leadership praxis, school districts, assistant principals' professional associations, universities, and regulatory bodies need to engage in coordinated efforts to address the problematic nature of the assistant principalship as an organizational leadership role and to institutionalize enabling supports and structures. Using suggestions from practicing assistant principals and the research literature, the following sections identify ways in which assistant principals' leadership passages can be scaffolded to increase the likelihood of professional and organizational success.

Reconfiguring the Assistant Principals' Role

New administrators experience the assistant principalship as a fragmented, punishing, and Sisyphean role because of its problematic configuration in policy and practice. According to Schmidt (2000), a role becomes problematic when:

> The purposes that different people invest in it are conflicting or contradictory; when they are far-ranging and limitless and virtually impossible to fulfill; when other people's defined expectations for the role and its purposes are at odds with one's own; when the ideal role is confronted by its actualities; and when the purpose one is meant to fulfill through the role are vague and undefined. (p. 831)

Assistant principals identify a pressing need for clear statements about the duties and boundaries of their role. They feel undervalued in their role, particularly when they are treated as firefighters and enforcers and when they experience conflicts, tensions, and ambiguities because their role lacks clear definitions and parameters (Armstrong, 2005; Marshall & Hooley, 2006). Under the current legal definition of "duties as assigned by the principal" (Brown, 2008), assistant principals are at the whim of their principal. Their role is configured as an institutional dumping ground for duties that veteran teachers, principals, and senior officers refuse to do. Unclear role boundaries expose newcomers to competing socialization demands which decrease their ability to exercise leadership and increase transitional burnout and alienation.

Effective administrator support cannot be achieved without an in-depth examination of, and changes to, the hegemonic institutional structures that maintain the assistant principalship as a subordinate, transitional role (Armstrong, in press-b). Organizational configurations of the assistant principalship as a temporary stepping-stone in the administrative passage are also problematic. They frustrate both the individuals who aspire to but are deemed ineligible for the principalship, as well as those who choose to remain in this position for personal or professional reasons. Furthermore, assistant principals who buy into the myth that they are in-transit are unlikely to challenge inequitable practices because of possible negative career impacts. This combination of practices introduces unnecessary complications within this organizational passage and ensures that needed professional and organizational changes do not occur.

Recommendations for Change

As part of fulfilling their articulated commitment to create equitable and democratic learning conditions, regulatory and training bodies need to work together to target the assistant principalship as a priority. Procedural and policy changes which reconfigure the assistant principalship as a substantive leadership role and connect it to school improvement and organizational change are critical. Assistant principals and their associations should be involved at all levels of dialogue. They should also play meaningful roles in determining the assistant principal's specific duties and responsibilities, as well as the curriculum, format, and delivery for their training.

Authentic conversations should be guided by critical questions related to the purposes and possibilities of the assistant principalship, its impact on assistant principals and their communities, and its possibilities for transformative leadership. These discussions should interrogate the following issues:

- What is the nature and purpose of the assistant principalship?
- What and whose purposes does it serve?
- How do policies, practices, and beliefs surrounding assistant principal transitions and socialization contribute to and perpetuate race/gender discrimination in recruitment, selection, and transition support?
- How can this role be changed to allow assistant principals to challenge and change systemic inequities?
- What leadership and management skills and competencies are needed? Who determines these skills? How will they be evaluated?
- How can we create a new story which honours the assistant principalship as a viable transformative role?

Failure to clarify and redefine this role will result in the continuation of reactive management approaches and hegemonic practices which discourage and alienate new administrators and disadvantage vulnerable school communities.

Enabling Supports and Structures

A number of researchers agree that the transition to the assistant principalship is a challenging process, and they stress the importance of timely and accurate information as well as early and on-going support (Hartzell et al., 1994; Marshall & Hooley, 2006; Sigford, 1998). Assistant principals often express frustration when they encounter disjunctions between pre-role training and on-the-ground realities of their role (Marshall & Hooley, 2006). In spite of ongoing recommendations, principal certification programs, as their title suggests, rarely acknowledge the assistant principalship or make distinctions between these two roles (Armstrong, in press-b). The following quote by Matthews and Crow (2003) suggests that principal certification courses may have limited relevance to principals as well:

> Frequently new administrators question the relevance of their university training in terms of specific work tasks that must be learned after they arrive in their first assignment. Others have pointed out that what effective university training has done for them is to provide the big picture and the innovative conceptions that sometimes get lost in the harried rhythm of the new administrator's work. (p. 264)

Technical-rational preparation models which focus solely on the principalship present a skewed vision of the organizational landscape. In addition to reinforcing hierarchical and static models of leadership, these transmission models are inadequate in preparing prospective assistant principals for the shifting dynamics of the administrative passage and the socio-emotional nature of transitions (Armstrong, 2004b, 2005). Administrative candidates may leave with the erroneous assumption that principals and assistant principals perform very similar roles and possess essentially equal powers. Assistant principals who enter their roles with unreasonable expectations as to the actual degree of authority and the scope of responsibility of that role are likely to experience additional ambiguities when they are confronted with the demands of middle-space roles and leadership/management tensions.

Recommendations for Change

Pre-service and in-service preparation programs need to work closely with school districts and professional associations to create coherent curricula, so that the disjunctions between professional and organizational socialization are reduced. As part of their curriculum redesign, these programs also need to reevaluate their underlying goals and purposes. Related important questions are:

- What are the tacit and unarticulated beliefs held by program developers and instructors about the assistant principalship?
- How do these assumptions shape professional socialization, discourse, and practice?
- How does the curriculum replicate dominant myths and hierarchies that reinforce the status quo?

- How can the curriculum prepare novices for organizational transitions and socialization?
- How can program developers and instructors work with school districts and professional associations to foster innovative leadership attitudes and practices that create ethical and socially just institutions?

Pedagogical Approaches and Content

Pre-service and in-service programs should be focused on intervention and prevention and premised on concerns of equity and social justice (Armstrong, in press-b; Marshall & Olivia, 2006; McMahon & Armstrong, 2006). Curricula should also be grounded in realities of school leadership and management with opportunities to acquire in-depth understandings of organizational theory. Critical and transformative approaches to administration that train leaders to deconstruct organizational realities, question the moral implications of policies and procedures, and co-construct democratic learning environments could form a necessary foundation for training (Foster, 2004; McMahon & Armstrong, 2006).

Aspiring and practicing administrators should be encouraged to critically analyze how and why organizational structures and administrative actions contribute to reproducing the status quo. Providing environments which facilitate discussion of issues related to effective leadership for growth and diversity can help newcomers develop the competencies required to build authentic partnerships with diverse stakeholders on behalf of students.

Courses should therefore be taught by professionals who are experienced in the assistant principal role, are well grounded in administrative theory, and have a critical perspective on school leadership. Professionals should help new and aspiring assistant principals acquire information and develop knowledge and skills related to:

- Assistant principals' articulated and enacted roles, duties, and responsibilities;
- The socio-emotional and physical demands of the assistant principalship;
- Transition and socialization challenges;
- The technical, emotional, and ethical tasks of middle-space leadership;
- Leadership for diversity and social justice;
- The impact of factors such as ability, race, economics, gender, and sexuality on educational practices and outcomes;
- School, district, and community structures and processes that support and/or hinder students at-risk, e.g., English language proficiency development and special education;
- The use and/or abuse of technology and data;
- Micro- and macro-organizational dynamics of schooling, i.e., how internal and external structures, politics, and power impact different levels of decision making and governance;
- Strategies that new assistant principals can use to successfully navigate organizational structures and foster ethical communities.

Blending Theoretical Knowledge and Practical Experiences

Middle managers and leaders need opportunities to practice exercising power and influence without undue reliance on formal authority to balance lateral, subordinate and superordinate demands, to think and act strategically, and to reflect on ethical action (Hartzell et al., 1994; Hill, 1992; Sigford, 1998). Studies of transformation processes (Daloz, 2000; Foster, 2004; Mezirow, 2000) also identify the following conditions as conducive to socially responsible democratic leadership: significant interactions and dialogue with others that construct a new we; conscious critical reflection that challenges earlier assumptions; a mentoring community where diversity and transformative discourse are encouraged; and opportunities for committed action that involve experiential learning opportunities.

Assistant principals' leadership development should include on-going apprenticeship and workshop opportunities that cultivate the management and leadership skills required at the different phases in the transitional cycle. Programs that integrate theory with opportunities for field practice, collaborative inquiry, case study analysis, self-study, individual and group dialogue, and feedback on performance, and action plans would lead to more critical and constructivist approaches to leadership. Experiential activities which are combined with in-class processes can promote deep learning and provide formal and informal opportunities for individual and group action.

Learning environments that facilitate engagement and practice must represent the target situations as closely as possible, provide behavioral models and coaching, opportunities for feedback, and gradually allow participants to take over their own learning (Meijers, 1998). The assistant principals identified the following components of their leadership development as important:

- Experiential learning opportunities in a variety of locations, e.g., job shadowing, internships and practica in a variety of schools and community settings;
- Safe spaces to reflect on their transition and develop new knowledge;
- Time to work with communities to build coalitions and to devise strategies for overcoming systemic inequities;
- Opportunities to develop hard and soft skills of leadership and management;
- Opportunities to observe and practice effective and democratic leadership approaches.

School Districts

Although district recruitment, selection, and placement processes represent important organizational opportunities for choosing democratic change agents, they are often premised on inefficient and inequitable processes which reinforce existing power structures. In many cases, assistant principals identify disjunctions between school districts' espoused commitments to new administrators and enacted practices which contribute to physical and psychological disengagement. Hiring and promotion are more dependent on existing support networks than on ability; minority candidates and those who challenge the system are often passed over in district rounds (Armstrong, in press-a; Marshall & Hooley, 2006). Inconsistencies in communicating promotion and placement information and personality and cultural mismatches between individuals, administrative teams, and schools increase transitional stress and strain.

Placing new assistant principals in difficult and unsafe working environments without support and training is unethical and needs to be addressed. School and district rites of passage which adopt "sink or swim" approaches that test new assistant principals' ability to endure administrative trials without complaint do not reflect the conditions or attitudes that would help novices learn to perform the role successfully. These practices encourage a survival of the fittest mentality which focuses newcomers' energies on their own basic needs, and they diminish their capacity to challenge inequities. While some may argue that most assistant principals weather the storm, these socialization practices contradict school districts' articulated mission and goal statements related to equity and social justice. They also misuse administrator expertise, increase alienation and resentment, promote physical and psychological disengagement, and militate against the kind of proactive leadership work required to improve schools.

Recommendations for Change

In order to meet the challenges of diverse, changing contexts, school districts need to recruit and hire energetic and thoughtful leaders and provide them with systematic, targeted, and ongoing professional support, and training. Central office supervisors need to say what they mean and do what they say if they wish to retain new leaders. This will require changes in recruitment and hiring practices as well as types and levels of support they provide to new assistant principals.

Promotion, Placement, and Hiring Practices

School district selection and placement processes represent an important opportunity zone for selecting future organizational leaders and modeling equitable practices. District leaders who are serious about redressing staffing inequities need to ask critical questions about their recruitment, hiring, and induction practices. How do we recruit and retain leaders who can make a positive difference for students and their communities? How do we create representative hiring? Who gets "tapped on the shoulder"? Why? Under which conditions? With what consequences? When asked how they would improve district hiring and promotion practices, the assistant principals provided the following suggestions:

• Transparent and equitable recruitment, hiring, and placement practices;
• Accurate job descriptions and role expectations;
• Matching of assistant principals' strengths to the needs and focus of the target school;

- Balancing the personalities and strengths of the administrative team;
- Timely and accurate information from immediate supervisors;
- Early support structures such as mentors, in-house buddies, and assistant principal support groups;
- Ongoing technical training, e.g., computers, data management and interpretation, scheduling, and policy implementation;
- Assistant principal succession planning which facilitates meetings and side-by-side mentoring with exiting assistant principals.

Induction, Mentoring, and Coaching

Assistant principals identify school district and professional association mentoring as critical to their success. Though well-intentioned, these interventions tend to be sporadic. Often falling short of their target to support newcomers, they do not provide time and space for assistant principals to integrate new skills and information. Freedman (1998) observes that new managers "need firm encouragement and support to fully experience (rather than deny) their own withdrawal process and to grieve and mourn the loss of their emotional attachment to these familiar, comforting competencies and responsibilities" (p. 5). New assistant principals also need ongoing support as they come to terms with the feelings of loss associated with giving up their former identity as a teacher and their membership within the teacher reference group. While making this shift in professional reference groups, they need reminders that shock, depression, and anger are common reactions to job losses. Providing information that helps them anticipate upcoming emotional challenges and time to develop new emotional and social anchors are also critical.

   Principals are often identified as key facilitators because of their power to assign duties and to structure activities that facilitate assistant principals' growth and leadership potential (Malone, 2001; Matthews & Crow, 2003). However, the area of principal mentoring needs to be explored in-depth. Critical discussions need to occur regarding how principals can effectively put these theoretical possibilities into practice. Given the current demands on principals, it is disingenuous to pretend that they have the time or capacity to support new assistant principals. In addition, higher-level creative problem solving and human resource development skills do not come naturally to all principals. In most cases, principal mentoring is haphazard, and its effectiveness varies by individual personality, skill, experience, and interest. Furthermore, assistant principals who are placed with new principals or in high-risk environments receive little support because their principals are also experiencing transitional challenges.

Recommendations for Change

Training and support bodies that provide administrative candidates and novices with the time, space, and emotional scaffolding to recognize identity and perspective changes and to resolve challenges can help them develop the kinds of administrative competence needed to lead today's schools. Where school districts and professional associations run parallel programs, concerted efforts must be made to create sustainable and coherent structures that are based on developmental approaches. Programs should be geared to newcomers' developmental needs, while building on the energy, enthusiasm, and commitment which they bring.

In order for newcomers to decipher how administrative work is socially constructed, they should be provided with the support of experienced trainers, mentors, and coaches. Trainer-mentors can work in conjunction with district professional development staff as coaches and critical friends who can support newcomers in building leadership capacity and developing administrative competence. These professionals should have a strong record of democratic action, experience with policy implementation, and an in-depth understanding of power dynamics of schools.

New assistant principals should be provided with space and support to mourn teaching losses, to establish their identity moors, to reflect on the changes they are experiencing, and to balance their personal and professional lives. External supports are critical during this period, particularly for administrators who are from traditionally underrepresented groups such as women and people of color, because of their limited access to the larger administrative network. Interventions such as personalized coaching, timely feedback on performance as well as structured and unstructured opportunities for individual and group discussion can help novices clarify their visions of educational leadership and construct viable administrative identities and practices. Particular emphasis must also be placed on the various aporias and challenges that typify the four epicycles and the cognitive, emotional, and social strategies that are required to resolve them. In addition to acquiring knowledge that can help them anticipate the psychological changes that accompany transformational processes, new and aspiring administrators should also be informed of the potential physical challenges and their vulnerability to stress. The following recommendations were also identified as important by new assistant principals:

- Time to critically reflect on their role and transition with other assistant principals;
- Support from principals and professionals who understand assistant principal roles;
- Training in how to work with high-risk populations;
- More staffing support, e.g., hall monitors and secretaries;
- Reduction in discipline tasks;
- Opportunities for curriculum leadership.

Aspiring and New Assistant Principals

Becoming an administrator is a powerful social and psychological journey that impacts newcomers on multiple levels and provokes unexpected behaviors and emotions. Just as institutions have an ethical obligation to facilitate one's passage, aspiring and novice assistant principals need to take charge of their own career development by preparing themselves as much as possible. When they look back on their transitions, new administrators often comment on the opportunities for learning that they missed. In order to reduce the shocks and surprises of this passage, aspiring and novice assistant principals must acquire information related to the role challenges and personal adjustments they are likely to encounter during their administrative passage, as well the culture and politics of their school and district. The following sections summarize key insights and suggestions that were provided by new assistant principals:

Professional Development and Learning

Becoming and being an assistant principal is an ongoing process that requires learning from others and one's personal experiences. In order to be effective leaders, aspiring and practicing assistant principals need to foster critical habits of mind and action frameworks that are grounded in deep reflection on self, role, systems, and society. Doing so will help them resist negative role definitions and immoral acts (Armstrong, in press-b). This can be achieved through formal and informal processes of inquiry, e.g., talking to practitioners, scholars and community members, taking courses, and reading about leadership transitions. In addition, they will need to:

- Find opportunities for formal and informal growth that will allow them to learn as much as possible about role transitions and passages and the expectations and demands of the assistant principalship.
- Learn from others' stories. Remember that each assistant principal's experience is unique. Although the voices of assistant principals who chose to leave the administrative profession are not discussed in this book, they are a valuable source of information regarding the reasons why good, well-intentioned individuals may relinquish this role.
- Listen to practicing and retired administrators' stories about becoming and being an assistant principal. Ask questions such as: Why were they motivated to become an assistant principal? What was their trajectory? What were their challenges? Who were the people that impacted their transition most? How did they navigate their school and district structures and politics? What were their key learnings? What would they do differently? As novices and candidates distill this information, they should try to identify common patterns and make connections with their own situations.
- Go through a process of self and external appraisal to determine suitability for the assistant principal role. This can be facilitated through self-assessment inventories and 360 degree feedback processes, self-reflective journaling, developing personal platform statements, as well as reflecting on and talking to mentors

about their goals, strengths, weaknesses, opportunities, and threats. Beginning and on-going questions for reflection and analysis could be: Why do I want to become an administrator? ("Getting out of the classroom" is not a good enough reason.) What are my short and long-term goals, needs, interests, and values? What kind of difference do I want to make? What are my potential losses? What sacrifices/compromises am I willing to make to achieve my goals?

- Develop familiarity with educational policies and structures that support students at the school and district levels, e.g., English language proficiency development, special education, guidance and counseling;
- Become familiar with issues related to personnel management, union contracts, finance, budget, and physical plant;
- Find out about the physical and psychological changes that accompany this transition;
- Stay in tune with the changes they are experiencing, as they go through the transition;
- Seek support, revisit platforms and plans, and refocus on their core goals and values.

Developing Networks and Sponsors

Aspiring and practicing administrators will find that networks and sponsors are important in facilitating their promotion and success as an administrator. Transitional needs will shift at the various stages of the administrative passage because of the difference between teaching and administrative work. This means that assistant principals must be actively involved in building multiple and appropriate networks that can support their socio-emotional passage. In order to overcome new challenges, aspiring and new assistant principals should:

- Ensure that they have different types of supportive relationships inside and outside of school that can counter the loss of their teaching identity and networks.
- Foster viable relationships with individuals at the vertical and horizontal levels of the organization that are built on trust and respect, e.g., make connections with administrators at the district and school levels, demonstrate leadership skills and an honest commitment to students.
- Seek advice from supervisors regarding how to navigate district processes, e.g., What are the selection, hiring, and promotion policies and practices? Are they willing to sponsor or support you? What kind of support are they willing to provide?
- Establish a strong base of critical friends undergoing similar transitions.
- Cultivate positive relations with experienced administrators inside and outside of their school who can understand leadership transitions, and who can provide appropriate support and advice.

Developing Administrative Skills and Competence

Becoming an administrator is a constantly evolving process of learning, being, and doing. New and aspiring assistant principals need to build technical skills, acquire knowledge about how their school and district works, and develop the physical, emotional and mental capacity to deal with the ongoing challenges of their role. Assistant principals recommend the following activities as important:

- Engage in meaningful projects that allow one to interact with others, build, and demonstrate leadership skills.
- Familiarize oneself with the technical infrastructure and needed skills prior to becoming an administrator. Where opportunities are available, become involved in developing student and staff schedules and timetables.
- Seek out opportunities to experiment with informal roles, e.g., chairing committees, doing attendance counseling, leading workshops in one's area of expertise. In addition to providing opportunities to improve one's communication, negotiation, and decision-making skills, these activities will allow a new or aspiring assistant principal to network with individuals outside one's department or unit.
- Apply for formal leadership roles at the school and district levels. Assuming a formal leadership role will contribute to one's development of a broader system perspective and provide opportunities to practice some of the tasks of administration.
- Find and cultivate role models that are congruent with one's goals and values.
- Actively seek out opportunities to shadow assistant principals whose work you respect so that you can learn about best practices.
- Take proactive steps to ensure good health and to balance one's personal and professional spheres.
- Celebrate milestones and successes.

Conclusion

This book raises a number of issues related to assistant principals' leadership and the nature of their role in the administrative hierarchy. The assistant principal's role is ignored and underused in the creation of effective and ethical school environments and this needs to change. Studies are required of the multiple roles that assistant principals must assume in order to be effective. A fine-tuned analysis of the phases of identity development is also needed. Theoreticians and practitioners need to work together to develop a clear articulation of this role and to examine its importance in creating student success and effective schools. This information would be useful in improving university and school district preparation and mentoring programs as well as assistant principal practices. Failure to provide the necessary social and psychological supports will lead to a reduction in educators applying for, and choosing to remain in, administrative positions.

The current boundaries around the assistant principalship restrict newcomers' leadership possibilities and perpetuate organizational hegemonies. As Ackerman and Maislin-Ostrowski (2002) contend:

> The leadership role that administrators assume shapes how they approach their practice, what they are able to accomplish, and how they think about their work; most important, it also shapes how they feel and believe the role permits them to feel. (p. 8)

However, the assistant principals' narratives show that despite the fact that current management efficiency paradigms constrain leadership praxis, William Foster's (1986) dictum that "leadership lies not in the position *given*, but in the position *taken*" (p. 15) still holds true. Although teachers enter the administrative landscape with the worthy intention of changing schools to benefit students, they often find that their avenues for ethical praxis are obstructed by hegemonic structures and policies that maintain the status quo. Their random acts of leadership provide testimony of missed opportunities, unintended consequences, and unfilled promises (Armstrong, 2004b).

Assistant principals' experiences highlight the need for coordinated approaches and interventions which address the problematic nature of their management role and prepare them for its intense socio-emotional, moral, and physical toll. School districts, universities, and regulatory bodies have a legal and moral obligation to provide working conditions that are conducive to sustainable administrative pathways and democratic and moral leadership. Failure to fulfill this promise will reinforce reactive approaches that punish vulnerable individuals and ensure the continued reproduction of system inequities that perpetuate unethical and ineffective practices (Armstrong, in press b).

Pathways and passages provide important developmental opportunities because of their potential to provoke individual and system growth (Armstrong, 2004b). The administrative transitions described in this book represent critical turning points for new assistant principals and their organizations that lead to important personal, professional, and organizational transformations. As new assistant principals navigate the crossroads between teaching and administration and progress through the various epicycles of their administrative journey, they consciously and unconsciously co-create personal and organizational pathways. Their choices carry important long-term ramifications, for themselves, as well as the communities to whom they owe a duty of care (Greenfield, 1993; Grogan & Andrews, 2002; Sigford, 1998).

Passages are interconnected webs of human interaction which carry an inherent potential to create vicious or virtuous cycles. The assistant principals' narratives show that vicious cycles perpetuate existing organizational metatnarratives, and reinforce custodial practices which harm newcomers and their communities. Virtuous cycles, on the other hand, foster ethical and equitable environments which support positive individual and organizational growth and transformation. Creating transformative cycles is a joint effort which is built on leadership imagination, hope, dedication, and action. This rests on the individual assistant principal's ability to achieve his or her dream to make a positive difference for his or her community. However, this cannot be achieved without a clear and consistent organizational commitment to creating pathways and stories which lead to equitable conditions and opportunities for all.

References

Abrego, P., & Brammer, L. (1992). Counseling adults in midlife career transitions. In H. Lea & Z. Leibowitz (Eds.), *Adult career development: Concepts, issues and practices* (pp. 235–254). VA: National Career Development Association.

Ackerman, R., & Maislin-Ostrowski, P. (2002). *The wounded leader: How real leadership emerges in times of crisis.* San Francisco, CA: Jossey-Bass.

Adams, J. (1976). Self-management. In J. Adams, J. Hayes & B. Hopson (Eds.), *Transitions: Understanding and managing personal change* (pp. 157–171). London: Martin Robertson.

Adams, J., Hayes, J., & Hopson, B. (1976). *Transitions: Understanding and managing personal change.* London: Martin Robertson.

Alvy, H. B., & Robbins, P. (1998). *If only I knew: Success strategies for navigating the principalship.* Thousand Oaks, CA: Corwin Press Inc.

Armstrong, D. (2002, May). *Administrative transitions: The journey from teacher to vice-principal.* Paper presented at the annual meeting of the Canadian Society for the Studies of Education, Toronto, ON, Canada.

Armstrong, D. (2004a). *Personal change and organizational passages: Transitions from teaching to the vice-principalship in a reform climate.* Unpublished doctoral dissertation, OISE/University of Toronto, Ontario, Canada.

Armstrong, D. (2004b). Constructing moral pathways in the transition from teaching to administration. *Values and Ethics in Educational Administration, 3*(1), 1–8.

Armstrong, D. (2005). Leadership at the crossroads: Negotiating challenges, tensions and ambiguities in the transition from teaching to administration. In H. D. Armstrong (Ed.), *Examining the practice of school administration in Canada* (pp. 113–128). Alberta, Canada: Detselig Enterprises.

Armstrong, D. (in press-a). Novice vice-principals: Betwixt and between the absurd contrasts of middle space leadership. In K. Anderson (Ed.), *The leadership compendium : Emerging scholars in Canadian educational leadership.* Fredericton, NB, Canada: Atlantic Centre for Educational Administration & Leadership.

Armstrong, D. (in press-b). Rites of passage: Coercion, compliance, and complicity in the socialization of new vice-principals. *Teachers College Record.*

Armstrong, D., & McMahon, B. (Eds.). (2006). *Inclusion in urban educational environments: Addressing issues of diversity, equity and social justice.* Greenwich, CT: Information Age.

Ashforth, B. (2001). *Role transitions in organizational life: An identity based perspective.* Mahwah, NJ: Lawrence Erlbaum Associates.

Ashforth, B., & Saks, A. (1996). Socialization tactics: Longitudinal effects of newcomer adjustment. *Academy of Management Journal, 39*(1), 149–178.

Banks, C. (2000). Gender and race as factors in educational leadership and administration. In *The Jossey-Bass Reader on Educational Leadership* (pp. 217–256). San Francisco: Jossey-Bass.

Begley, P. (1999). Value preferences, ethics, and conflicts in school administration. In P. T. Begley (Ed.), *Values and educational leadership* (pp. 237–254). New York: State University of New York.

Begley, P. (2003). In pursuit of authentic school leadership practices. In P. T. Begley & O. Johansson (Eds.), *The ethical dimensions of school leadership* (pp. 1–12). Boston: Kluwer Academic.

Blackmore, J. (2002). Leadership for socially just schooling: More substance and less style in high-risk, low-trust times. *Journal of School Leadership, 12*, 198–222.

Brammer, L. (1981). Intervention strategies for coping with transitions. *Counselling Pychologist, 9*(2), 19–36.

Brammer, L. (1991). *How to cope with life's transitions: The challenge of personal change.* Washington: Hemisphere.

Bridges, W. (1980). *Transitions: Making sense of life's changes.* Toronto: Addison-Wesley.

Bridges, W. (2001). *The way of transition: Embracing life's most difficult moments.* Cambridge, MA: Perseus.

Bridges, W. (2003). *Managing transitions: Making the most of change* (2nd ed.). Cambridge, MA: De Capo.

Brown, A. (Ed.). (2008). *Ontario education statutes and regulations.* Toronto, Ontario: Carswell.

Brown, D. (1995). A values based approach to facilitating career transitions. *The Career Development Quarterly, 44*, 4–11.

Bullogh, R., Knowles, J., & Crow, N. (1991). *Emerging as a teacher.* New York: Routledge.

Burbules, N. (1997). Aporia: Webs, passages, getting lost, and learning to go on. *Philosophy of Education.* Retrieved July 31, 2003, from http://www.ed.uiuc.edu/EPS/PES-yearbook/97_docs/burbules.html.

Bush, T. (2003). *Theories of educational leadership and management* (3rd ed.). Thousand Oaks, CA: Sage.

Butler, E. (1998). Alcohol use and abuse as a rite of passage. *Reaching Today's Youth, 3*(1), 18–23.

Calebrese R. (1991). Effective assistant principals: What do they do? *NAASP Bulletin, 75*(533), 51–57.

Calebrese R., & Tucker-Ladd, P. (1991). The principal and assistant principal: A mentoring relationship. *NAASP Bulletin, 75*(533), 67–25.

Cantwell, Z. (1993). School based-leadership and professional socialization of the assistant principal. *Urban Education, 28*, 49–68.

Clandinin, D., & Connelly, F. (1994). In N. K. Denzin & Y. S. Guba (Eds.), *Handbook of qualitative research* (pp. 413–427). London, UK: Sage Publications.

Clandinin, D., & Connelly, F. (2000). *Narrative inquiry: Experience and story in qualitative research.* San Francisco: Jossey-Bass.

Clegg, T., Kornberger, M., & Pitsis, T. (2005). *Managing organizations: An introduction to theory and practice.* Thousand Oaks, CA: Sage.

Cobb, K. (2005). *The Blackwell guide to theology and popular culture.* Boston, MA: Blackwell.

Cole, A., & Knowles, J. (2000). *Researching teaching: Exploring teacher development through reflexive inquiry.* Toronto: Allyn & Bacon.

Conway, J. (1990). Organizational rites as culture markers of schools. *Urban Education, 25*(1), 195–206.

Cooper, J. (2002). Constructivist leadership: Its evolving narrative. In L. Lambert, D. Walker, D. Zimmerman, J. Cooper, M. Lambert, M. Gardner, et al. (Eds.), *The constructivist leader* (pp. 112–126). New York: Teachers College.

Cranton, P. (2006). *Understanding and promoting transformative learning: A guide for educators of adults.* San Francisco: Jossey-Bass.

Crow, G., & Grogan, M. (2005). The development of leadership thought and practice in the United States. In F. W. English (Ed.), *The Sage handbook of educational leadership: Advances in theory, research, and practice* (pp. 362–379). Thousand Oaks, CA: Sage.

Daloz, L. (2000). Transformative learning for the common good. In J. Mezirow & Associates (Eds.), *Learning as transformation: Critical perspectives on a theory in progress* (pp. 103–123). San Francisco: Jossey Bass.

Dotlich, D., Noel, J., & Walker, N. (2004). *Leadership passages: The personal and professional transitions that make or break a leader.* San Francisco: Jossey-Bass.

Earl, L., Freeman, S., Lasky, S., Sutherland, S., & Torrance, N. (2002). *Policy, politics, pedagogy and people: Early perceptions and challenges of large-scale reform in Ontario schools.* Toronto, Ontario: ICEC, University of Toronto.

Fein, M. (1990). *Role change: A resocialization perspective.* New York: Praeger.

Felner, R., Farber, S., & Primavera, J. (1983). Transitions and stressful life events: A model for primary prevention. In R. D. Felner, L. Jason, J. Moritsugu & S. Farber (Eds.), *Preventative psychology: Theory, research and practice* (pp. 199–220). New York: Pergamon Press.

Fineman, S., Sims, D. & Gabriel, Y. (2005). *Organizing and organizations* (3rd ed.). Thousand Oaks, CA: Sage.

Fishbein, S., & Osterman, K. (2001). *Crossing over: Learning the ropes and rules of the teacher-administrator relationship.* Paper presented to the annual meeting of the American Educational Research Association, Seattle, WA, April 10–14, 2001. (ERIC Document Reproduction Service No. ED 463276).

Foster, W. (1986). *Paradigms and promises: New approaches to educational administration.* New York: Prometheus Books.

Foster, W. (2004). The decline of the local: A challenge to educational leadership. *Educational Administration Quarterly, 40*(2), 176–191.

Freedman, A. (1998). Pathways and crossroads to institutional leadership. *Consulting Psychology Journal: Practice and Research, 50*(3), 131–151.

Gardner, H., Csikszentmihalyi, M., & Damon, W. (2001). *Good work: When excellence and ethics meet.* New York: Basic Books.

Gillborn, D., & Ladson-Billings, G. (2004). Introduction. In G. Ladson-Billings & D. Gillborn (Eds.) *The Routledge Falmer reader in multicultural education: Critical perspectives on race, racism, and education* (pp. 1–4). London: Routledge.

Gillborn, D., & Youdell, D. (2000). *Rationing education: Policy, practice, reform and equity.* Philadelphia: Open University.

Glaser, B., & Strauss, A. (1971). *Status passage.* Chicago: Aldine.

Glesne, C., & Peshkin, H. (1992). *Becoming qualitative researchers: An introduction.* White Plains, NY: Longman.

Goffmann, E. (1959). *The presentation of self in everyday lofe.* New York: Anchor Books.

Gold, M., & Douvan, E. (1997). *A new outline of social psychology.* Washington, DC: American Psychological Association.

Goodman, D. (2001). *Promoting diversity and social justice: Educating people from privileged groups.* Thousand Oaks, CA: Sage.

Greenfield, W. D. (1977). Administrative candidacy: A process of new role learning. *Journal of Educational Administration, 15*(1), 30–48.

Greenfield, W. D. (1985a). *Being and becoming a principal: Responses to work contexts and socialization processes.* Paper presented to the annual meeting of the American Educational Research Association, Chicago IL, April 2, 1985. (ERIC Document ED 254 932).

Greenfield, W. D. (1985b). The moral socialization of school administration: Informal role learning outcomes. *Educational Administration Quarterly, 24*(4), 99–119.

Greenfield, W. D. (1985c). Studies of the assistant principal: Toward new avenues of inquiry. *Education and Urban Society, 18*(1), 7–27.

Greenfield, W. D. (1993). Articulating values and ethics in administrator preparation. In C. A. Capper (Ed.), *Educational administration in a pluralistic society* (pp. 267–287). Albany, NY: State University of New York.

Greenfield, W. D. (1995). Toward a theory of school administration: The centrality of leadership. *Educational Administration Quarterly, 31*(1), 61–85.

Griffith, A. (2001). Texts, tyranny and transformation: Educational restructuring in Ontario. In J. Portelli & R. Solomon (Eds.), *The erosion of democracy in education: From critique to possibilities* (pp. 83–98). Calgary, Alberta: Detselig.

Grogan, M., & Andrews, R. (2002). Defining preparation and professional development for the future. *Educational Administration Quarterly, 38*(2), 233–256.

Hagestad, G. (1991). Trends and dilemmas in life course research. In W. R. Heinz (Ed.), *Theoretical advances in life course research* (pp. 23–57). Bremen: Deutscher Studien Verlag.

Hart, A. (1991). Leadership succession and socialization: A synthesis. *Review of Educational Research, 61*(4), 451–474.

Hart, A. (1993). *Principal succession: Establishing leadership in schools.* New York: SUNY.

Hartzell, G. (1991). Induction of experienced assistant principals. *NAASP Bulletin, 75*(53), 75–83.

Hartzell, G. (1993). Effective leadership - When you're not at the top. *The High School Magazine, 1*(2), 16–19.

Hartzell, G., Williams, R. C., & Nelson, K. T. (1994). *Addressing the problems of first-year assistant principals.* Paper presented at the annual convention of the National Association of Secondary School Principals, February 19, 1994. (ERIC Document ED 369 179).

Heck, R. (1995). Organizational and professional socialization: Its impact on the performance of new administrators. *The Urban Review, 7*(1), 31–49.

Hill, L. A. (1992). Becoming a manager: Mastery of a new identity. Boston, MA: Harvard Business School Press.

Hopson, B., & Adams, J. (1976). Towards an understanding of transition: Defining some boundaries of transition dynamics. In J. Adams, J. Hayes & B. Hopson (Eds.), *Transition: Understanding and managing personal change* (pp. 3–26). London, UK: Marin Robertson.

Hoyle, E., & Wallace, M. (2005). *Educational leadership: Ambiguity, professionals and managerialism.* Thousand Oaks, CA: Sage Publications.

Kegan, R. (2000). What form transforms? A constructive-developmental approach to transformative learning. In J. Mezirow & Associates (Eds.), *Learning as transformation* (pp. 35–69). San Francisco: Jossey-Bass.

Kincheloe, J. L. (2003). *Teachers as researchers: Qualitative inquiry as a path to empowerment* (2nd ed.), London: Routledge Farmer.

King, K. (2005). *Bringing transformative learning to life.* Malabar, FL: Krieger.

King, T. (2003). *The truth about stories: A native narrative.* Toronto: Anansi.

Kwan, P., & Walker, A. (2008). Vice-principalship in Hong Kong: Aspirations, competencies and satisfaction. *School Effectiveness and School Improvement, 19*(1), 73–97.

Lambert, L. (2002). Toward a deepened theory of constructivist leadership. In L. Lambert, D. Walker, D. Zimmerman, J. Cooper, M. Lambert, M. Gardner et al. (Eds.), *The constructivist leader* (pp. 34–62). New York: Teachers College.

Leithwood, K., Fullan, M., & Watson, N. (2003). *The schools we need: Recent education policy in Ontario and recommendations for moving forward.* Toronto: OISE/UT.

Leucke, R. (2003). *Managing change and transition.* Boston, MA: Harvard Business School.

Levin, J. (1999). *The poetics of transition: Emerson, pragmatism, & American literary modernism.* London: Duke University.

Louis, M. R. (1980). Surprise and sense making: What newcomers experience in entering unfamiliar settings. *Administrative Science Quarterly, 25,* 226–251.

Louis, M. R. (1981). Career transitions: Varieties and commonalities. In R. E. Hill, E. L. Miller & M. A. Lowther (Eds.), *Adult career transitions: Current research perspectives.* Michigan: University of Michigan.

Major, D. (2000). Effective newcomer socialization into high-performance organizational cultures. In N. M. Ashkanasy, C. P. Wilderom & M. Peterson (Eds.), *Handbook of organizational change* (pp. 355–383). London: Sage.

Malone, R. 2001). Principal mentoring. *Eric Digest, 149,* 1–6.

Marris, P. (1974). *Loss and change.* London: Routledge & Kegan Paul.

Marshall, C. (1985a). Professional shock: The enculturation of the assistant principal. *Education and Urban Society, 18*(1), 28–58.

Marshall, C. (1985b). Facing fundamental dilemmas in education systems. *Education and Urban Society, 18*(1), 131–134.

Marshall, C. (1992a). The assistant principalship: An overview of the frustrations and rewards. *NAASP Bulletin, 76,* 88–94.

Marshall, C. (1992b). *The assistant principalship: Leadership choices and challenges.* California: Corwin Press.

Marshall, C. (1993). *The unsung role of the career assistant principal.* VA: National Association of Secondary School Principals.

Marshall, C., & Greenfield, W. (1987). The dynamics of the enculturation and work of the assistant principal. *Urban Education, 22*(1), 36–52.

Marshall, C., & Hooley, R. (2006). *The assistant principalship: Leadership choices and challenges* (2nd ed.). Thousand Oaks, CA: Corwin.

Marshall, C., & Mitchell, B. A. (1991). The assumptive worlds of fledgling administrators. *Education and Urban Society, 23*(4), 396–415.

Marshall, C., & Olivia, M. (2006). *Leadership for social justice: Making revolutions in education.* New York: Pearson.

Matthews, J., & Crow, G. (2003). *Being and becoming a principal: Role conceptions for contemporary principals and assistant principals.* Boston: Pearson Education.

McMahon, B., & Armstrong, D. (2006). Framing equitable praxis: Systematic approaches to building socially just and inclusionary educational communities. In D. Armstrong & B. McMahon (Eds.), *Inclusion in urban educational environments: Addressing issues of diversity, equity and social justice.* Greenwich, CT: Information Age.

Meijers, F. (1998). The development of a career identity. *International Journal for the Advancement of Counselling, 20,* 191–207.

Meijers, F. (2002). Career learning in a changing world. *International Journal for the Advancement of Counselling, 24,* 149–167.

Merriam, S. B. (1998). *Qualitative research and case study applications in education.* San Francisco: Jossey-Bass.

Merriam-Webster Online Dictionary. Retrieved December 9, 2008, from http://www.merriam-webster.com/dictionary/passage.

Mezirow, J. (2000). Learning to think like an adult: Core concepts of transformation theory. In J. Mezirow & Associates (Eds.), *Learning as transformation: Critical perspectives on a theory in progress* (pp. 3–33) San Francisco: Jossey-Bass.

Michel, G. (1996). *Socialization and career orientation of the assistant principal.* South Carolina: South Carolina State University, Department of Education. (ERIC Document Reproduction Service No. ED 395 381).

Morgan, A., & Drury, V. (2003). Legitimizing the subjectivity of human reality through qualitative research method. *The Qualitative Report, 8*(1), Retrieved June 2, 2003, from http://www.nova.edu/sss/QR/QR8-1/morgan.html.

Nanavati, M., & McCulloch, B. (2003). *School culture and the changing role of the secondary vice principal.* Research report prepared for the Ontario Principals' Council, December 2003. Toronto, Ontario, Canada: Ontario Principals' Council.

Nicholson, N. (1990). The transition cycle: Causes, outcomes, processes and forms. In S. Fisher & C. L. Cooper (Eds.), *On the move: The psychology of change and transition* (pp. 83–105). Chichester, UK: John Wiley & Sons.

Nicholson, N., & West, M. (1988). *Managerial job change: Men and women in transition.* Cambridge, UK: Cambridge University.

Nicholson, N., & West, M. (1989). Transitions, work histories and careers. In M. B. Arthur, D. T. Hall & B. S. Lawrence (Eds.), *Handbook of career theory* (pp. 181–201). Cambridge: Cambridge University Press.

O'Connor, D., & Wolfe, D. (1991). From crisis to growth at midlife: Changes in personal paradigm. *Journal of Organizational Behavior, 12,* 323–340.

Olson, L. A. (2000). The nature of the assistant principalship in relation to the principalship. *GSU Educational Forum, 5,* 7–12.

Oshry, B. (1993). Converting middle powerlessness to middle power: A systems approach. In T. D. Jick (Ed.), *Managing change: Cases and concepts* (pp. 401–412). New York: Irwin McGraw-Hill.

Playko, M., & Daresh, J. (1993). Mentoring programs for aspiring administrators: An analysis of benefits to mentors. *ERS Spectrum*, 12–16.

Radnor, H. (2001). *Researching your professional practice: Doing interpretive research*. Philadelphia: Open University Press.

Rodriguez, A. (2002). Redefining our understanding of narrative. *The Qualitative Report*, 7(1), Retrieved March 1, 2002, from http://www.nova.edu/sss/QR/QR7-/rodriguez.html.

Rusch, E. (2004). Gender and race in leadership preparation: A constrained discourse. *Educational Administration Quarterly*, 40(1), 14–26.

Ryan, J. (2003). *Principals and inclusive leadership for diverse schools. Studies in educational leadership*. Hingham, MA: Kluwer.

Saks, A., & Ashforth, B. (1997). Organizational socialization: Making sense of the past and present as a prologue for the future. *Journal of Vocational Behavior*, 51, 234–279.

Saks, A., & Ashforth, B. (2000). The role of dispositions, entry stressors, and behavioral plasticity theory in predicting newcomers' adjustment to work. *Journal of Organizational Behavior*, 21, 43–62.

Schein, E. (1978). *Career dynamics: Matching individual and organizational needs*. Reading, MA: Addison-Wesley Publishing.

Schlossberg, N. (1981). A model for analyzing human adaptation to transition. *The Counseling Psychologist*, 9(2), 2–18.

Schmidt, M. (2000). Role theory, emotions, and identity in the department headship of secondary schooling. *Teaching and Teacher Education*, 16, 827 842.

Schmidt, L., Komski, G., & Pollack, D. (1998a). *Novice administrators: Personality and administrative style changes*. Illinois. (ERIC Document Reproduction Service No. ED 427387).

Schmidt, L., Komski, G., & Pollack, D. (1998b). *Novice administrators: Psychological and physiological effects*. Illinois. (ERIC Document Reproduction Service No. ED 427386).

Schultz, E., & Lavenda, R. (1987). *Cultural anthropology: A perspective on the human condition*. St. Paul, MN: West.

Schwandt, T. A. (2000). Three epistemological stances for qualitative inquiry: Interpretism, hermeneutics, and social construction. In N. K. Denzin & Y. S. Guba (Eds.), *Handbook of Qualitative Research* (2nd ed., pp. 189–213). London: Sage Publications.

Scoggins, A., & Bishop, H. (1993). *A review of the literature regarding the roles and responsibilities of assistant principals*. Paper presented at the annual meeting of the Mid-South Educational Research Association, New Orleans, November 10–12, 1993. (ERIC document ED 371 436).

Sheehy, G. (2006). *Passages: Predictable crises of adult life*. New York: Ballantine.

Sigford, J. (1998). *Who said school administration would be fun? Coping with a new emotional and social reality*. Thousand Oaks, CA: Corwin.

Simpson, P. R. (2000). *Assistant principal's survival guide: Practical guidelines and materials for managing all areas of your work*. Paramus, NJ: Prentice Hall.

Spector, P., & Fox, S. (2002). An emotion-centered model of voluntary work behavior: Some parallels between counter productive work behavior and organizational citizenship behavior. *Human Resources Management Review*, 12, 269–292.

Taylor, E. (2000). Analyzing research on transformative learning theory. In J. Mezirow & Associates (Eds.), *Learning as transformation: Critical perspectives on a theory in progress* (pp. 285–328). San Francisco: Jossey-Bass.

Trice, H., & Beyer, J. (1984). Studying organizational culture through rituals and ceremonies. *Academy of Management Review*, 9(4), 653–669.

Trice, H., & Morand, D. (1989). Rites of passage in work careers. In M. B. Arthur, D. T. Hall & B. S. Lawrence (Eds.), *Handbook of career theory* (pp. 397–416). Cambridge: Cambridge University Press.

Tzu, L. (2009). In *Brainy Quote*. http://www.brainyquote.com/quotes/authors/l/lao_tzu.html.

Van Gennep, A. (1960). *The rites of passage*. Chicago: The University of Chicago Press.

Van Maanen, J., & Schein, E. H. (1979). Toward a theory of organizational socialization. In B. M. Shaw (Ed.), *Research in organizational behavior* (pp. 209–264). Greenwich, CT: JAI.

Viney, L. (1980). *Transitions: The major upheavals most women must face and how they experience them*. Victoria: Cassels Australia.

Walker, D. (2002). Constructivist leadership: Standards, equity and learning – weaving whole cloth from multiple strands. In L. Lambert, D. Walker, D. Zimmerman, J. Cooper, M. Lambert, M. Gardner, et al. (Eds.), *The constructivist leader* (pp. 1–33). New York: Teachers College.

Williams, T. (2001, August). *Unrecognized exodus, unaccepted accountability: The looming shortage of principals and vice-principals in Ontario public school boards*. Ontario, Canada: Ontario Principals Council.

Wollon, M. & Sommer, S. (2003). *Saying farewell: Management as a performance art*. Retrieved June 1, 2006, from http://www.ux1.eiu.edu/~cfmlw2/048POB.pdf.

Young, R., & Collin, A. (Eds.). (1992). Constructing career through narrative and context: An interpretive perspective. In *Interpreting career: Hermeneutical studies of lives in context* (pp. 1–14). London: Praegar.

Index

Lightning Source UK Ltd.
Milton Keynes UK
18 December 2009

147711UK00001B/54/P